If you have ever needed a reset button in life, *Dare to Begin Again* is the book for you! It is an encouragement to pick up the pieces and start over again with God's help. This book is a how-to manual on rebuilding your life, your hopes, and your dreams. Rosalinda brings the stories of other overcomers to life through the lens of Scripture. It's not over—as she says, "God's still writing your story."

—*Dr. Ed Hindson*
Author and host, *The King Is Coming* telecast
Distinguished professor, Liberty University, Lynchburg, VA

Who would have guessed that you can be delighted and delivered by the same beautiful words?! I was instantly drawn in by the way in which Rosalinda wraps words of truth around the reader—making profound revelations simple to understand and comforting to hear. This book has it all! The author gives you so much to chew on and talk over as you process—it would be ideal for a women's ministry book club or for just a few of your favorite girlfriends.

—*Amie Dockery*
Director of Women's Ministry, Covenant Church, Dallas, TX
Co-Author, *On Daddy's Shoulders*
Speaker, Flourish Women's Ministry

Page after page, Rosalinda Rivera shows us that beginning again doesn't have to mean starting over. No matter where you are in life, no matter what you've gone through, *Dare to Begin Again* will help you pick yourself up right where you are and propel you toward your dreams.

—*Victor Torres*
Founder, New Life For Youth and New Life International
Author, *Victor* and *Reaching Your Addicted Loved One*

I love it! Literally from the introduction of this book, Rosalinda is sharing huge, life-changing truths. If you've ever been hurt, disappointed, or stuck, you will find healing and practical ways to move forward in *Dare to Begin Again*!

—*Martha Munizzi*
Recording artist and Dove Award-winner, *Change the World*

Rosalinda Rivera has written a must-read book for anyone who may be questioning what in the world to do next. *Dare to Begin Again* is funny, uplifting, and absolutely life-changing. I encourage everyone to read this book!

—*Keisha Cory*
Worship leader, Hope City United Church, Albany, GA
Recording artist, *Still Standing*

Rosalinda Rivera is a powerful speaker who hits the heart and stimulates the mind with her transforming messages. Go deeper with her when you read *Dare to Begin Again*. Don't miss a page, as she both encourages and challenges you to step into all God has waiting for you. This is a must-read book. No matter what you've been through or where you are today, this message will lift you up and set you on a course for a future full of promise and purpose. *Dare to Begin Again* is a game-changer.

—*Anita Agers Brooks*
Inspirational life coach and international speaker
Author, *Getting Through What You Can't Get Over*

It's challenging to offer hope to those who've been told, "You'll never change." Rosalinda does it beautifully. Through her own experiences and those of women she's helped, Rosalinda highlights the miraculous transformation made by Christ alone. Reading, you'll be encouraged that in Christ, you can begin again.

—*Dr. Mark Becton*
Senior pastor, Grove Avenue Baptist Church, Richmond, VA

Dare to Begin Again is an encouraging guide to starting over. It is full of real-life examples for those of us who want to learn from our past and embrace the future. Rosalinda brings biblical examples, real-life stories, and her trademark humor to the table in this life-changing book.

—*Shirley W. Mitchell*
Author, *Fabulous After 50*

Do we dare to dream when our lives seem hopeless? Rosalinda Rivera reminds us of the power of prayer and faith when life is heavy and hard to take. She shares true stories to encourage others who may be facing difficult decisions and personal crises. A timely word for our world today!

—*Karen Jordan*
Author, *Words That Change Everything*

LET GOD WRITE YOUR BEST FUTURE

DARE TO BEGIN Again

ROSALINDA RIVERA

WHITAKER
HOUSE

Except where otherwise indicated, all Scripture quotations are taken from the *Holy Bible, New International Version*®, NIV®, © 1973, 1978, 1984 by the International Bible Society. Used by permission of Zondervan. All rights reserved. Scripture quotations marked (ASV) are taken from the American Standard Edition of the Revised Version of the Holy Bible. Scripture quotations marked (KJV) are taken from the King James Version of the Holy Bible. Scripture quotations marked (ESV) are taken from *The Holy Bible, English Standard Version*, © 2000, 2001, 1995 by Crossway Bibles, a division of Good News Publishers. Used by permission. All rights reserved. Scripture quotations marked (NASB) are taken from the *New American Standard Bible*®, NASB®, © 1960, 1962, 1963, 1968, 1971, 1972, 1973, 1975, 1977, 1988 by The Lockman Foundation. Used by permission. (www.Lockman.org). Scripture quotations marked (NLT) are taken from the *Holy Bible, New Living Translation*, © 1996, 2004, 2007 by Tyndale House Foundation. Used by permission of Tyndale House Publishers, Inc., Carol Stream, Illinois 60188. All rights reserved.

All dictionary definitions are taken from *Merriam-Webster's 11th Collegiate Dictionary*, electronic version, © 2004.

DARE TO BEGIN AGAIN:
Let God Write Your Best Future

Rosalinda Rivera
www.rosalindarivera.com
www.newlifeforyouth.com
rosalindarivera1@gmail.com

ISBN: 978-1-64123-096-4
eBook ISBN: 978-1-64123-097-1
Printed in the United States of America
© 2018 by Rosalinda Torres Rivera

Whitaker House
1030 Hunt Valley Circle
New Kensington, PA 15068
www.whitakerhouse.com

Library of Congress Cataloging-in-Publication Data (Pending)

No part of this book may be reproduced or transmitted in any form or by any means, electronic or mechanical—including photocopying, recording, or by any information storage and retrieval system—without permission in writing from the publisher. Please direct your inquiries to permissionseditor@whitakerhouse.com.

1 2 3 4 5 6 7 8 9 10 11 ᴜᴊ 25 24 23 22 21 20 19 18

DEDICATION

To the love of my life, Carlos, and
our beautiful children: Alana, Gabriel, and Victor.

CONTENTS

INTRODUCTION

Welcome, friend. Although we've just met, I have something important to ask you:

IS YOUR LIFE WHERE YOU WANT IT TO BE?

If your answer is no, then this book is for you.

An unavoidable truth is this: there will be bumps and bruises along life's path. Some of them are unfair, uncalled for, and unjustified. It stinks, I know. Sometimes, things just don't work out the way we thought they would.

But I have great news: it doesn't have to stay that way. God is a God of new beginnings, and throughout the entire Bible, we read about people who were stuck, disappointed, and faced impossible situations, people God freed.

If you are reading this, you're breathing, alive, and motivated. You've decided not to stay stuck where you are, but to move forward. You're motivated to do great things, to realize the dreams that once kept you up at night, to let your heart hope for things long forgotten.

I understand that beginning again sounds like it takes a commitment. The truth is, it does. But you won't be alone. I'll be right with you, walking through the pages of this book.

I'm not promising immediate benefits. But I will say that if you put your heart into the process, you will see change and with that change, hope.

You might say, "This sounds very encouraging and exciting, but I'm not sure how to pick up and begin again."

LET ME OFFER SOME PRACTICAL TIPS:

1. *Ask the Lord to do what you cannot do*, to take care of the situations you've struggled with, to teach you how to let go. I'm not saying you will magically forget all the pain, disappointments, and hurt. But if you never forgive yourself or others, you will stay bound in a spiritual shackle. You will remain stuck.

2. *Disconnect.* Are there some people you need to unfollow on social media? Give yourself permission to move beyond toxic people, habits, and situations. Remaining addicted to unhealthy connections keeps you stuck. Change your route—don't drive by old memories. Past habits are not getting you any closer to your healing.

3. *Find a safe accountability partner.* Having someone share your desire to begin again will help you move forward faster. If you feel alone, join a local church; if you already belong to one, try attending a meeting of any of the small groups it may offer. Groups like Weight Watchers are successful because they realize the power of togetherness. Call someone when you're having a bad day. Connect with a friend who will encourage you when you make the right choices. A strong support system can help you unstick and move you toward your greater purpose.

4. *Be transparent.* Stop trying to act like someone you're not. The authentic you is the best you. Many times, we hold ridiculous expectations over our own heads. Stop

being your own worst critic. Set your goals and be realistic about your expectations. Understand that falling is not failure. Problems exist only when you don't get back up again or try to wear a mask.

You're closer than you think to getting past uncomfortable situations, and moving into the destiny that God has called for you.

One thing you'll learn about me is this: what you see is what you get. And with that comes the truth. Sometimes it hurts, other times it's a relief, but truth will always set you free. God penned this promise in John 8:32.

You might be tempted to put the book down at this point. I understand—change can be scary. But I dare you to keep on reading because your best days are ahead of you. Make a decision today that you will not let your past define you. Decide in this moment that you will not let your hurt keep you stuck.

Growing up, I had athletic coaches who spoke into my life. I needed them. I didn't always like them or what they had to say in the moment, but I am forever grateful that when I was ready to quit, they pushed me on. They made me run one more lap, do one more sit up, pushed me through exhaustion, one more time. Even when I was tired, fed up, or hurting, they wouldn't let me quit.

During this time, think of me as your coach. Together, you and I will go through this journey. You have someone cheering you on as you decide to begin again. I will also push you to do more than you think possible, when necessary.

There is light at the end of your tunnel. There is victory in your tomorrow. Stop complaining about your current situation and let's do something about it. I dare you to turn your story over to God. I dare you to begin again.

Chapter 1

BEGIN AGAIN

What would it mean for you to begin again?

At first glance, you might not think I understand the desire to make a fresh start, but I get it in a very real way. First glances never tell the whole story—certainly not God's story.

I grew up in a world where we were surrounded by street people. They were our neighbors, friends, and often our house guests. Many of the people I knew came from a world of gangs, drugs, and prostitution. You may have heard of *The Cross and the Switchblade.*[1] I knew people from that world.

Through the years, as a child and an adult, I've seen more than twenty thousand people come off those streets and do what once seemed impossible. Actually, it *was* impossible through their own efforts. But because they dared to begin again and allowed God to start writing their stories instead of continuing on their own, they found new lives.

I've watched people start over, make fresh starts, and allow their Creator to reset their lives. They're people whose tales of transformation prove God is still at work. He's written and re-written their life's chapters—and He's willing to do the same for you.

---

1. David Wilkerson, John and Elizabeth Sherrill, *The Cross and the Switchblade* (New York: Berkley Publishing Group, 1962)

Don't believe me? Then hang tight because I'm going to show you through true stories and practical applications how all things are possible when we let Christ give us strength. Take it from a girl who knows.

I want you to understand that after it seems you've reached your end, God's not done with you yet. In this book, not only will I share true stories from others (with their permission, of course), but I'll also share some of mine. As you will learn, I understand how it feels to go through something you will never get over.

> AFTER IT SEEMS YOU'VE REACHED YOUR END, GOD'S NOT DONE WITH YOU YET.

WHAT WOULD IT LOOK LIKE FOR YOU TO BEGIN AGAIN?

+ Would you move to a different location?
+ Would it mean a complete body overhaul?
+ Would it mean digging up a dream you buried long ago?
+ Would you dare to make yourself vulnerable?
+ Would you allow someone to get close and risk a love relationship?
+ Would it mean getting out of your rut?
+ Would you finally forgive yourself?

If you are looking for hope, encouragement, and support, or if you need to start life over, then read on. I've written this book for you.

Believe me, friend, you can begin again!

A few years ago, when I turned on the garbage disposal, I knew immediately from the chunking sound that something wasn't right. A call to a local plumber revealed the source of brokenness.

Somehow, my wedding ring was in the machine, tearing up the motor, and breaking my heart. Friend, you know I was having a heart attack. That ring meant the world to me. It represented everything between me and my man. The loss of this important symbol of love and commitment to my husband upset me. Nothing consoled me. All I wanted was my precious ring back.

Two weeks later, as I walked through the mall, I passed a jewelry store. It felt like a large magnet was pulling me into the store. You know that bling was calling my name. My motive was innocent, but then the situation took a turn.

A particularly stunning ring drew me in. The sales clerk reached into the case and reverently handed it to me. As I studied the center stone's facets, I thought about the miracle of God's creation when He made diamonds. It took a lot of pressure to transform raw rock into precious jewels. Someone had to dig them out of the ground to expose their beauty. Have you ever thought about how a dirty rock with maybe a glimmer of shine becomes a sparkling, faceted gem?

Can you see each rough stone scooped up and tossed into a dusty bin, lost in a crowd of other dirty rocks? I imagine some of us feel like that at times—I know I have. I know the people I help through our ministry have felt like that.

But that day, as I studied the ring in my hand, I thought about the center stone. I imagined a master jeweler picking it up out of a heap. With tender care and gentleness, the crust and grime would have been dusted off its exterior. He or she would have looked through a jeweler's loop at the unique clarity and crystal direction hidden at its core. They would have artfully cut away its flaws. Finally, the jeweler must have polished it till it gleamed, before proudly presenting it to the world.

Our Master wants to do that with us.

Another customer asked the clerk a question, and in an instant, I did something without thinking. I slipped that diamond ring on my finger. It slid on like it was made just for me. I held my hand up and said, "Oh, my goodness!" Let me tell you, that bling took my breath away. The jeweler had done great work...and here's where my problem began. Lost in my thoughts, I didn't notice the swelling in my finger.

Come on, y'all, we have all done crazy things like that. But this time, I really did it. I was hoping I could get that gorgeous ring off my finger before anyone noticed what had happened.

I turned away and began to wiggle the ring. I hoped I could rock it off my finger. But no matter how hard I tried, it was not happening. Neither was keeping my efforts a secret.

The sales lady's voice made me jump. "Is everything okay?"

I tried to play it off. "I just wanted to see how it looked on my finger."

She smiled in that polite, "Okay, but I'm not really buying that" way. But at least she stepped aside, continuing to help another customer. She didn't move far; I did have that rock on my finger, after all. And by the expression on her face, she was trying to figure out what I was up to.

Although the humorous scene wasn't lost on me, my mind went into panic mode: My husband is going to kill me. He's about to buy me the ring of my dreams and he doesn't even know it.

My mind raced a hundred miles a second. In my imagination, I saw the store clerk sawing my finger to remove the ring. I hoped the handcuffs wouldn't hurt too badly when they hauled me off.

While my inward panic increased, outwardly, I pretended I had the situation under control. In desperation, I held my hand straight up in the air and acted as if I was still checking out the ring. The saleswoman stepped back toward me.

"Look at that glimmer," I said loudly enough for her to hear, but quietly enough not to attract more mall onlookers. There were enough people in the store watching already.

The clerk kept coming, so I added, "This ring does look good on me." It stopped the saleswoman's approach, but she kept watching.

Feeling desperate, I felt the beads of sweat dripping off my face. I held my arm above my head. I pretended to admire the ring from a few different angles, but what I really thought was the blood might drain, causing my finger to shrink.

I prayed silently, "Dear God in heaven, let this swelling subside." But the puffiness in my finger refused to diminish.

After seeing no change and feeling embarrassed, I conceded defeat. I motioned to the sales lady, who was still eyeballing me from a few feet away. Holding back a nervous laugh, I gushed, "I'm so sorry! I only wanted to try it on to see what it would look like on my finger. But it's stuck. I can't get it off."

She reached across the counter. In a manner that spoke business, though not roughly, she grabbed my hand. After a quick exam, she said, "I'll be right back."

A couple of minutes later, she returned with a bag of ice and a spray bottle of glass cleaner. I understood the ice, but the glass cleaner confused me. It didn't take long for me to realize that she'd done this before.

She rubbed my finger with the ice above and below the ring, front and back, then sprayed my finger.

Bam! The ring loosened and immediately came off. I was free!

THE TRUTH IS, WE ALL GET STUCK SOMETIMES.

Until my release, whether the ring was stuck on my finger or my finger was stuck in that ring, the fact is, I was stuck.

The truth is, we all get stuck sometimes. Like my decision to slip the ring on my finger, we sometimes make thoughtless choices. Many lead us into situations that get us stuck.

+ Maybe you feel you are stuck in a job that's going nowhere.

+ Perhaps you're in a marriage where you feel no love.

+ Maybe you feel you are stuck spiritually or financially.

+ You may feel like you're in a rut and the reality is, time is ticking.

Thoughts go through your mind like, *My life should be better than this by now.* Or, *Why haven't I saved any money to get a better car?* You scold yourself for dealing with the same things you've dealt with for years. Your shame says, I should have overcome this by now. It's like you're ankle deep in mud.

If you can relate to anything I've just said, I have some great news for you. It might be hard for you to believe this, but you truly are not alone. In fact, most of the greatest heroes in the Bible experienced great failures, too. Many were stuck once, just like you.

> MOST OF THE GREATEST HEROES IN THE BIBLE EXPERIENCED GREAT FAILURES, TOO.

Here are just a few examples:

+ The man at the Pool of Bethesda was stuck in paralysis.

+ Naomi was stuck in bitterness.

+ The man in the graveyard was stuck with his demons.

+ Daniel was stuck in the lions' den.

+ Joseph was stuck in a pit.

+ Jonah was stuck in a whale.

+ Moses's mother was stuck in grief.

+ Jacob was stuck on a girl.

+ Hannah was stuck in sadness.

+ David was stuck in a cave.

+ The Samaritan woman at the well was stuck in habit.

+ Lazarus was stuck in a tomb.

+ Gideon was stuck on a concept.

+ Peter was stuck in fear.

+ Mary was stuck in loss.

+ Paul was stuck in prison.

These are people whose histories we will explore in depth. But for now, let me remind you that while they were stuck, God was still writing their stories. So if you're stuck, consider this: you are in good company. Your potential greatness is only waiting for His pen.

> YOUR POTENTIAL GREATNESS IS ONLY
> WAITING FOR HIS PEN.

While they felt trapped, God developed greatness in these biblical and historical heroes. He saw past their current circumstances and viewed them through His jeweler's loop. He dug them out of the dirt and picked them out of the crowd. He dusted off their crusts and grime, and artfully cut away their flaws. He transformed each of them into unique and useful polished gems. His work took time. But during seasons of pain and fear while they faced the unknown, God consistently whittled away their rough edges. The Master got them *unstuck.*

He will do the same for you—if you dare to believe and start paying attention to the way He's already working in your life. As I learned in my younger years, sometimes He shows up through the ordinary and mundane.

I went to college in Cleveland, Tennessee. It was quite beautiful, with mountains as far as the eye could see. But the longer I lived there, the more I noticed this horrible odor. No one who lived in the area ever mentioned it, but I could sure smell it.

The smell was so rotten, I felt like gagging, particularly on the days it rained. I asked myself, Am I crazy? Am I the only one who smells this?

When I finally asked my friends from the area if they noticed the stench, they said, "Oh, we're used to it. There's a paper plant in town and when it rains, it gets worse. It's just normal to us. We don't even think about it."

The people in the community were accustomed to the paper factory's fumes. They simply learned to live with it. They accepted it as an ordinary part of their lives.

So, can we get real for a minute?

Sometimes, we're like the people who live near the paper factory. We learn to exist with a smell in our lives. So let me ask you: do you have something that stinks in your life? Your relationships? Your job? Your finances?

Without realizing it, you can allow stinky circumstances to become your norm. If you want to begin again, you have to determine *why* a fresh start is important. If you don't believe your own goal is valuable, you won't follow through with it. And no one else is going to make the change for you.

Right now, I dare you to shake off the acceptance that's holding you back. Draw a line in the dirt of your situation and repeat after me:

I am a victor, not a victim. I am courageous and strong. I refuse to believe the enticement of the enemy who wants me to stay stuck in my current situation. It's time to *begin again*. I am worth it. Jesus paid the price and I will stop shifting the blame. I am done with excuses.

People throughout the ages have wanted to escape something—myself included. There have been times in my life when I was stuck. One question arises: How can I begin again?

For example, let's look at the details of a story you may know. In the timeless pages of the Bible, God shows us an example of a man who was desperately stuck—for thirty-eight years.

THE PARALYZED MAN WAS STUCK FOR 38 YEARS

In John 5:1–15, a paralyzed man sat by the Pool of Bethesda. It was likely under one of the five porches where lame, blind, or paralyzed people waited in hopes of a miracle. The Pool of Bethesda, in both ancient and modern times, symbolizes healing. It was a place where people flocked when they needed a breakthrough. And after suffering with immobility for thirty-eight years, let me tell you, this man was desperate.

Can you imagine how this paralyzed man must have felt? Most likely, people either gawked at him or passed him by, treating him as if he and his condition were invisible. Can you relate? Have you ever felt invisible? Or contrariwise, have you ever felt like a spectacle on display?

The Bible goes on to say that Jesus saw the man and knew he had been ill for a long time. Anyone who observed the man would have known he was stuck in a chronic circumstance, imprisoned by his own body.

Jesus asked him an interesting question in verse 6: Does he want to get well?

What kind of question was that? The man was at the pool of healing, after all. Only sick people went to the Pool of Bethesda.

At certain times, an angel came and stirred up the water. Then the first person who entered the pool was instantly made well. Wasn't it obvious the man both needed and wanted healing? Let's face it: it must have required great effort for a man with paralysis to make it to the pool in the first place.

The man told Jesus, *"I have no one to help me into the pool when the water is stirred. While I am trying to get in, someone else goes down ahead of me"* (John 5:7).

He's saying, "Hey, this is not my fault. No one is helping me and I can't get into the water when it's in healing mode anyway because someone gets there before me. I'm stuck in this condition."

He was a blame shifter. Instead of listening to the question Christ asked, the man's immediate response was to complain. Instead of plunging into the pool, he plunged into excuses.

What about you? What do you say about your circumstances today? Are you making excuses or do you really want to be made well? Are you so used to your situation that you hardly notice it? Maybe you blame someone else for where you are today. It's so easy to fall into that trap. Until I learned to stop playing the blame game, I was stuck, too.

I want to challenge you to stop blaming others and stop making excuses. Smother the temptation to point your finger at someone else. We have to stop blaming before we are free to begin believing.

WE HAVE TO STOP BLAMING BEFORE
WE ARE FREE TO BEGIN BELIEVING.

If you spend your time and energy focused on all of the reasons someone else is at fault, you will never allow yourself to start over. On the contrary, it may keep you stuck in the muck, only pulling you down deeper.

To begin again, you have to want it—enough that you're willing to act.

So how did Jesus get the paralyzed man unstuck? And what can you apply to your situation?

"Then Jesus said to him, 'Get up! Pick up your mat and walk'" (John 5:8).

What the Lord commanded the man to do may not initially make sense. His words sound simple for a healthy man, but for a man struck with paralysis? Can you imagine the thoughts running through this guy's head? *Jesus, are you crazy? I can't get up. I can't walk.* But he had a decision to make: Am I going to do it the old way, which hasn't worked for thirty-eight years, or will I follow Jesus?

Frankly, the man had little to lose—his old way of being stuck wasn't working out so hot.

This is where faith comes in.

When your plans are not working out, it's time to change your strategy. When what you're doing is not moving you closer to your goal, it's time to move in a different direction. Your internal GPS needs an update. If you wonder whether to stay put or get up, measure your decision against the history of your success or lack of it.

You have two choices: never come out of your pain or sorrow and remain in your place of dissatisfaction; or obey. Rise up. Pick up the bed you've made. And walk.

Let God direct your steps. This man by the pool was waiting on a couple of things. He had convinced himself that these things had to happen in order for him to receive wholeness. But Jesus had a different plan. Thank you, Jesus!

Jesus made him toss out that idea that hadn't worked for the past thirty-eight years. He wasn't going to find his healing by waiting by the pool for a chance that might never come. Jesus offered a new way.

What about you? Have you obeyed God's voice or have you talked yourself out of believing He might heal you? So often, we want a full explanation of God's plan. We want to compare His plan to our own, missing the miracles right in front of us. His ways are not our ways—not even close.

My husband had a saying for our children when they were growing up: "Partial obedience is disobedience." He wanted them to understand that doing half the plan would not get them the full reward. Another reminder we used to tell our kids was, "Don't think about it; don't hesitate; just do it."

As children with a limited view of life, they didn't always see how obedience would benefit them. But as parents, we knew the path to what works was clear.

We are God's children and our loving Father is looking for our full obedience so He can lead us to a place of healing. He isn't looking for back talk, endless questions, or a mountain of excuses. He simply wants us to believe Him and obey.

When Scripture makes something clear to us, we just need to do it. We need to obey.

Let's clarify something here: The Bible won't provide a chapter and verse telling you to pick up the pieces of your life and start over in California. It doesn't specify where you will find the person you're meant to marry. But if you are wondering how to begin again, commit yourself to sitting in silent moments of prayer. Bring your needs before the Lord. Read the Bible and listen as God speaks to you through His Word. Trust that He will answer.

In time, you will hear His voice. The Holy Spirit will give you a feeling in your heart. He will show you signs, bring you to passages of Scripture, or speak to you through others. He will ultimately tell you what to do, for as Romans 8:14 says, *"For those who are led by the Spirit of God are the children of God."*

Every day, I get alone with God and take a moment in silence. For me, it's in the morning before I turn on my electronics, social media, or even an ear to my own family. For you, it might be during your lunch break or before you go to bed. What's important is that you intentionally spend time with Him. I ask His Holy Spirit to guide me because I learned a long time ago, His ways are definitely better than mine.

By meeting with God on a regular basis, I've discovered the secret to getting to know Him well. Much like my other close relationships, I hang out with Him often. We chat over coffee, lunch, or dinner. There came a point where He was so familiar, I recognized His voice. I don't need to see Him face-to-face; I've spent enough time in His presence to know exactly who He is when He speaks. And I trust what He has to say.

That's what happens when we take time to talk with the Lord. The more we read His Word, the more familiar His voice becomes. It's comforting to know that we don't have to do life alone. When we have His Spirit to guide us and His Word, the Bible, to light our path, we have assurance. It's never too late for us to begin again.

For you to begin again, you must believe that the end result will make the transformation process worthwhile.

> ALLOW GOD TO TURN THE ROCK THAT IS YOU INTO THE SPARKLING DIAMOND YOU WERE MEANT TO BE.

So here's the deal: if you don't believe it's possible, you won't become and do all you were made for. You must allow God to turn the rock that is you into the sparkling diamond you were meant to be. If you don't, you will stay stuck. He is the master jeweler, and He sees your inner worth, hiding beneath whatever is holding you back. God is willing to help you begin again. I praise God that I'm no longer who I was because I dared to allow God to help me begin again. So my question for you, my friend, is this:

WILL YOU DARE?

At the end of each chapter, I'm going to offer you a set of D.A.R.E.'s. I designed these statements to make you think, challenge you, and offer you hope. As you read on, I'm also going to delve into your hidden hopes, secret desires, and buried talents. Get ready...get set...and let's go!

I D.A.R.E. YOU TO BEGIN AGAIN

Decide: Stop watching others live while you stay stuck. Listen to God and decide to rise. Decide to pick up your bed. Decide to walk.

Allow: Let go of your ways, your thoughts, and your plans—and turn them over to God. Accept that His plans may look different from your own.

Rise: What is the last thing you remember God telling you to do? Choose to act on it. Even if it's one tiny step, move toward obedience.

Enjoy: Ask God to show you the blessings you have now, as you trust Him to write the rest of your story. He isn't done with you yet. Remember, just because your every day doesn't feel good doesn't mean there isn't something good in your every day.

Chapter 2

DREAM AGAIN

You haven't met me face-to-face, so you don't know how insanely in love with Jesus I am. I mean, seriously, what an amazing concept that He would lay down His life for me and you! But even more, that He would plant dreams in our hearts. That He would resurrect us from dead lives. That He would lift us to heights greater than anything we could imagine, in spite of the mess we made yesterday.

Because of Him, we get to begin again. I don't know how you feel about Him, but I am forever grateful.

I see the proof of His love and power every day. I'm the executive director over the men's and women's programs at New Life For Youth[2], a ministry started by my dad, Victor Torres, and my mom, Carmen. Dad came from a gang life where he ran the streets of *The Cross and the Switchblade*. As you can imagine, I understand real redemption. Dad's youth was so raw and his salvation so dramatic, it was recently made into a movie, *Victor*.[3] I love that I was able be a part of bringing my dad's story to the big screen by being an associate producer on that project.

I was born with a servant's heart, but God refined it through the conditioning that began early in my life. Today, I minister with

2. http://newlifeforyouth.org
3. http://www.thevictormovie.com

my parents, along with a tall, dark, handsome, and fine pastor named Carlos. He's my husband, my friend, and my man. Early on, he taught me Latin dancing, and let's just say that twenty-two years later, he still sweeps me off my feet.

I am also the mother to three beautiful children: Alana, gifted with a gorgeous singing voice; Gabe, a young man motivated to lead the next generation; and Victor, who at age twelve is passionately pursuing his gift of entrepreneurship.

Most of my life has centered on serving others, but can I lay something down right now? Between us? At times, I've wrestled with the question, "What does God have for me?"

> AT TIMES, I'VE WRESTLED WITH THE QUESTION,
> "WHAT DOES GOD HAVE FOR ME?"

You know what I mean?

I'm used to telling other people, "God has a healing in store for you. He's offering you hope. The Maker of the universe wants to lift you out of that depression. You think your story is over, but stop accepting the status quo. Let me interrupt that thought, because God isn't through with you—He's still writing your story."

Sometimes, I need someone to speak that kind of encouragement to me. I need my own reminder to get ready for an encounter with the presence of God, the kind of life-altering, Holy Spirit encounter that shakes you out of feeling sick and tired. Even if I have to say it to myself, I need to hear, "My story isn't over yet!"

On July 23, 2009, I felt excited as I anticipated my trip to North Carolina. Driving to a conference for writers and speakers, I was following my dream. But I was also obeying as I answered a call God had placed over me. This journey was my opportunity to confidently step out in faith.

Shortly after my return from the conference, doors began to open. I was on my way to fulfilling a vision I knew wasn't seeded by me—God had planted it in my heart. It was one of those pinch-me-is-this-real? moments.

When I returned home, I ran into my house so excited and there was Carlos, grinning from ear to ear. He knew I was like Cinderella—the shoe finally fit. His words were perfect: "Babe, go after your dreams."

Further confirmation came as I watched lives change. It felt so good to be a vessel for God's work. I rode the wave…until….

Ninety days later, the U.S. economy began to decline. Carlos and I suffered a great loss in our personal business. We had to put our house up for sale. We went from donating to the food bank to depending on it.

Stress took over my life. I had three electrocardiograms in three months. I struggled as my weight climbed and my health declined. My ministry screeched to a halt, but my responsibilities as a servant forced me to soldier on. I couldn't stop, my family needed me, especially my dad. Do you know what I'm talking about? Those times when trials come, one after another after another? It's in those times that we can feel the waves crashing over us, taking us down to what could be our bottom.

About twenty-four months after the chaos started, the work on the movie about my dad's life began. Little by little, my attention and energy splintered. Between home, family, work, and this enormous project, though I loved every minute, I felt stretched. Although I was tired, I pushed through. I had expected to put in some extra hours, not yet understanding the hours would turn into years. I'm sure you can think of a time when you've felt so stretched.

Mostly, I told myself I was fine with the situation. I remember saying to Carlos, "I think it's over; the season of my dreams has passed, but I'm okay with it."

Liar, liar…

In the silent, private moments, I whispered the truth. "God, I thought it was time."

While time passed and my fatigue grew, I felt discouraged and exhausted. As I focused on my surroundings, I wished things were different. I believed God called me to inspire people to dream again. I felt a burning desire to help them live life out loud. But when my mind drifted to my own dreams, I'll admit there were definitely times of discouragement.

I soon started throwing pity parties for myself. And not the kind with a violin playing somber music in the background. No, I had an entire orchestra playing dirges. I whined toward heaven. "I'm so busy helping my husband, my kids, my dad, my mom, and the people in our ministries. But what about me? I do enjoy helping other people experience the reality of their dreams coming true. But what about mine?"

Does this sound familiar?

Then the guilt took over where the melancholy left off. I must have been wrong. I guess God didn't really speak to me. It must have been my own mind making things up. Why should I dare to dream? I'm causing myself unnecessary pain to think God has something special planned for me. It is what it is. Deal with it, Rosalinda. You had your time, short as it was. It's over.

But then God shook me out of my feeling sorry for myself, why-is-this-happening-to-me, sad-sack state. While I wallowed, He was planning a surprise.

In the middle of a conference I attended, it happened. While I sat, not out loud, but in the stillness of my soul, I heard God speak to me: "You are pregnant with twins."

My response was, *What?! You've got to be kidding me. Don't play with me, Jesus. That's why I'm gaining weight?*

I know, I know, that wasn't a super spiritual reaction.

As I continued to listen, I knew God wasn't telling me about a literal pregnancy. Instead, He told me, "Though you feel as if your dreams are fading away, honor Me by first helping your dad and mom. The second twin, your personal ministry, will come only after the first, your dad's movie, is born. But get ready, for when the time is right, I will open doors for you that you can't even imagine."

I immediately began to sob, as His promise shook me to the core. I felt both broken and emboldened, having experienced an uncommon presence of God.

In the following months, I traveled for my dad's movie and worked hard. I had some great days and met fantastic people. I felt blessed and honored. I was also excited for the promised birth, the one that God had whispered to my soul. And then, it happened.

In the span of seven days, I took many deep breaths while flying to Los Angeles, Texas, and Nashville. The final meeting lasted eight hours, but at its conclusion, the movie deal was done. I boarded the escalator, went to my room, fell on my bed, and wept, as a flood of exhaustion and emotions overtook me. I had kept my word and brought the first twin into the world. I knew I was finally free to once again pursue my dreams. The book you are holding is part of that second twin.

Your past experiences may not mirror mine, but maybe you can relate to some of my feelings. Have you had hopes and dreams that you feel have been delayed? At times, I felt hopeless as I wrestled with what was, in spite of what I wished for—when it felt as if my window of opportunity had passed.

NAOMI'S LIFE LOOKED HOPELESS...

I wonder if that's how Naomi felt. She was familiar with sadness, resentment, and bitterness. In the Bible's book of Ruth,

Naomi's life looked pretty hopeless, but then again, God wasn't finished with her story.

Naomi lived in Bethlehem, a small village stamped with a promise, although nothing in Bethlehem looked promising at the time because there was a famine in the land. So Naomi and her family relocated to Moab. She must have felt excitement and anticipation. But then, tragedy hit, and Naomi had to bury her husband, Elimelech.

Things must have seemed a bit better when Naomi's two sons got married. I'm a mama of two boys, so I imagine Naomi must have been happy to welcome her daughters-in-law. The wine surely flowed with the music. Who knows? Naomi may have even danced.

Like any good, single mother, Naomi took care of her kids. She probably couldn't even mourn properly because she had to be the strong one, shouldering as much as possible, to spare her children added grief. Maybe you can relate.

Ten years pass. Naomi probably laughs again. She likely celebrates any good things that come her way. She might even dance once more. Then the unthinkable happens. Naomi loses not just one son, but both of them.

The kind of sorrow Naomi must have felt is the kind most women fear. The gut-wrenching, soul-piercing, emotionally paralyzing pain of losing your husband and your children. I imagine she cried out in agony, "My God, my God, my husband is dead and now you've taken my boys! Why? What have I done to deserve this kind of punishment? Do you hate me that much? Are you there? Are you listening? Do you care?"

No wonder she wanted to change her name to Mara, meaning bitter. I'd feel bitter, too. Actually, I've felt bitter over far fewer problems than Naomi's.

In the dark silence of grief, Naomi may have felt as if God abandoned her. But the truth was, despite appearances, she was not alone. And, there was still purpose left in her life. Her future held more than she could envision in her present. God wasn't done writing Naomi's story. And God's not done writing yours.

Somehow, when there was nothing left inside her, out of sheer resolve and will, Naomi dares to take in one more deep breath. She decides to go back to Bethlehem. Her dutiful daughters-in-law come with her. She must have thought, *They would be better off staying in Moab with their families.* So she tried to convince them to go back.

One left but the other, Ruth, stood her ground and told her mother-in-law:

> *Don't urge me to leave you or to turn back from you. Where you go I will go, and where you stay I will stay. Your people will be my people and your God my God. Where you die I will die, and there I will be buried. May the* Lord *deal with me, be it ever so severely, if even death separates you and me.*
>
> (Ruth 1:16–17)

In essence, Ruth was telling Naomi that she loved her as her own dear mother and would not abandon her for the world.

The Bible says Ruth "clung" to her mother-in-law. And this is where God begins to change Naomi. Although she couldn't see how this chapter would end, God was already writing the rest of her story with His pen of promise.

The clouds of sorrow drift away, allowing the sun to shine again on the two women who had lost everything. Ruth's refusal to compromise paid off. She maintained her integrity and self-respect, until she found a man who was worthy of her love, a *"mighty man of wealth"* named Boaz, who was a kinsman of Naomi's husband.

As the story of Ruth unfolds, Naomi is the catalyst that God used to bring about a positive change. Her past bitterness didn't stop her usefulness. God redeemed it all.

> ## NAOMI TAUGHT RUTH TO WAIT ON GOD, EVEN WHEN ALL HOPE SEEMED LOST.

Naomi was the voice of wisdom God used to bring about the new hope, life, and love both women desired. She taught Ruth to wait on God, even when all hope seemed lost. She spoke with godly wisdom and taught the younger woman to wait for her Boaz, versus trying make something happen out of another dead-end situation.

What about you? Are you called to be a Naomi? Or maybe you need to listen to Naomi's voice. Don't miss your Boaz trying to make things happen on your own. Whatever your circumstances, God holds the pen of promise in His hand for you. He will keep His word. He is still writing your story.

GOD HAS A GREATER PLAN FOR YOUR LIFE

You may feel discouraged, hurt, or even bitter, but God hasn't given up on you. He has a greater plan for your life.

+ Maybe you want to go back to school. If so, take heart, God is still writing your story.

+ Maybe you're struggling with your weight. I've got good news: God is still writing your story.

+ Maybe you're single. Don't stop waiting for your Boaz. God's still writing your story.

+ Maybe you're widowed. Keep looking for your Ruth, someone to speak wisdom to, because God is still writing your story.

+ Maybe your marriage is on the rocks. Don't jump ship. God's still writing your story.

+ Maybe you're divorced. Pick up the pieces, and move on. God is still writing your story.

+ Maybe you think your dreams have died. Dig them out of their grave, because God's still writing your story.

+ Maybe you believe it's too late. Rebuke that lie—God is still writing your story.

I know what it feels like when your dreams begin to fade away. It happens to most people at some point in their lives. We have a vision, a plan, goals, a target...then the unexpected happens. If we aren't careful, we fall prey to the illusion that God broke His promise. He abandoned us. He did forsake us.

> IF WE AREN'T CAREFUL, WE FALL PREY TO THE ILLUSION THAT GOD BROKE HIS PROMISE.

Little by little, we begin to think God only keeps His promises for others. Complacency sets in. We justify our lack of action and excuse ourselves from moving forward. Our dreams begin to wither. Our hope begins to die.

I went through a season where I didn't feel strong or significant. I stopped believing God's word was true for me. Some of you will understand.

You have your own reasons why life ripped away your dreams or pushed pause on your passions. Life is not always fair. When life becomes too painful to hang on to our desires, we must not allow our dreams to fade away, like a town we've passed by on the highway of life.

YOU HAVE A CHOICE

Don't allow negative thoughts to enter your mind and anxiety to take control. The enemy wants to tear down what God is building in you and through you. Satan knows where to attack. He's an expert at crafting anxious thoughts out of unknown futures. But this is not what God desires from your story.

> SATAN IS AN EXPERT AT CRAFTING ANXIOUS THOUGHTS OUT OF UNKNOWN FUTURES.

Our Almighty, Sovereign God wants you to know that the enemy's end is already written. The father of lies is defeated. That's the rest of God's story. You are free indeed, but you must dare to believe.

You can begin again, not because of your own power or will, not because you can talk yourself into a positive state of mind, but because God is with you. He is your comfort, your strength, and your willing guide. God alone holds the pen of promise over your life. But He may ask you to march into the enemy's camp and take back what was stolen.

As long as there is breath in your lungs, you have a purpose and it's not too late. There are two important dates on a tombstone: the day of our birth and the day of our death. We can't change those dates, but we can change what happens between them.

Don't give up on your dreams. Stop believing your desires won't work out for you. Quit saying things will never get better. Don't let discontent disconnect you from God's truth. Through Christ, you lack nothing, so you have everything you need to begin again.

You may know this truth already and perhaps part of your purpose is to encourage someone else, because you know what it feels like to walk out of a valley.

Even if life doesn't look so promising for you right now, God is going ahead of you. He prepares the way where it seems there is no way. He already sees the difficulties you will face and He is right there by your side.

Psalm 23 is a Bible chapter often used at funerals. Pastors use it to mark the end of life with peace, but in reality, it makes much more sense for those of us still alive.

This psalm begins with a powerful promise: The Shepherd leads those who follow Him to a place where they lack nothing. When we accept Him, Jesus is our shepherd, and everything we need is provided through Him. He leads us by still waters and refreshes our souls.

GOD PREPARES THE WAY WHERE IT SEEMS THERE IS NO WAY

I hope you are getting this because everything you need to begin again will be provided.

When things in our life get out of hand, when things break down, when tragedy strikes all around, God is with us. Faithfully. We can count on Him to never abandon or forsake us. He is fully aware of our weaknesses; He understands our desire to give up; He even knows when we need something as simple as rest. And He offers it without condition or pressure.

Psalm 23 tells us that God is our guide. Though some of us will face life's darkest valleys, there is no need to fear, because God is with us. He is our Comforter and never makes us walk alone.

God can see into the future and He's already written our victory. He's even prepared a meal for us in the presence of our enemies. Finally, because of this great promise He has penned, God makes our blessings overflow. Throughout our lives, His goodness and love will stay with us on our best days and on our worst days. We can rest in the security of His presence, daring to dream again.

Through His Word, the Bible, the Lord declares a promise over you. According to Revelation 3:7, He has opened doors that no one can close and closed doors that no one can open. These are "God gets all the glory" kind of doors.

If you have accepted His Son, Jesus Christ, as your savior, God has declared His favor over your life. He will go before you and after you; He is above you and below you. His Spirit dwells inside you.

No matter what you have experienced, or what is happening around you now, God planted a dream in your heart. And you have not missed your opportunity. Your story is not over! God affirms this.

> *"For I know the plans I have for you,"* declares the LORD, *"plans to prosper you and not to harm you, plans to give you hope and a future."* (Jeremiah 29:11)

This is not a promise meant for someone else; this is a promise for you. Regardless of the source of your issues—whatever followed you from your childhood, anything that derailed you, whatever the core hurt that caused you to act out or shut down—I dare you to believe. I dare you to dream. In the next chapter, in order to begin again, I will dare you to release. In God's story, you are a slave no more.

I D.A.R.E. YOU TO DREAM

Decide: Stop hiding behind complacency. Decide to dig up your dreams and believe God's call on your life.

Allow: Accept that God has more in store for you. You can't see it now, but that doesn't mean He isn't writing a greater purpose into your next chapter.

Rise: What negative messages do you need to crumple up and throw away? Rise above the labels, the naysayers, the lies, and any words holding you back. Stop letting others define you. God's story for your life is the only one that matters.

Enjoy: Let yourself dream again. Write down those ideas, brainstorm creative concepts, and draw up some plans. Lay your hopes before God and tell Him the desires in your heart. You won't surprise Him—He's the one who wrote them into your DNA. We make Him smile when we step out in faith to dare to dream again.

Chapter 3

RELEASE AGAIN

Have you ever been trapped? In a car, on a plane, in an elevator, under a person, inside a building?

I have—and I hate the feeling of helplessness when you are so stuck you can't break loose. Between you and me, it makes me crazy. I'd do just about anything to get unstuck.

I will never forget the day the doctor sent me to have an MRI after a back injury. That day, my life changed forever. Though I'd never suffered from claustrophobia before, it settled over me like a blanket of oppression.

My budget was tight, so they sent me to an outpatient clinic. When I walked into the building, I was surprised by how modern and beautiful the lobby was. I thought to myself, *This place looks as great as the main facility—the one that would have cost an arm and a leg.* The nurse called my name and escorted me out of the building into a mobile unit. I knew I was in trouble when I saw the mobile-sized smaller machine. But she assured me I would survive, and even tried to soothe my concern by offering me a headset. I'm not sure what she thought this headset was going to accomplish, but unless there were blinders, too, this was not going to go well. As I lay completely confined, with my arms pinned against the inner walls of the chamber, I began to cry out to Jesus like never before.

The light disappeared. It only took about ten seconds before I could feel my breathing quicken and my heart pump harder. I tried to fight the feeling, but no amount of self-talk worked; my mouth refused to listen to my brain. Before I knew it, like a small child screaming for help, I heard myself yelling at the nurse. "Get me out! Get me out!"

But the nightmare did not end that day.

Later that night, and for the next two months, I suffered from night terrors, all with that sense of entrapment. I dreamt I fell into a deep well and couldn't scale the sides. I dreamt I locked myself in my car and couldn't get the doors open. A myriad of places held me captive and in every dream, all I wanted was freedom.

To this day, I sleep with the door open and prefer the windows in my house open as well. A natural extrovert, I now feel squeamish if I get stuck in the middle of large crowds. Every time I get into an elevator, I look up at the ceiling and immediately formulate a plan. I can even hear the *Mission Impossible* theme song in my head. I practice in my mind how to maneuver my way out through the ceiling if the need arises.

> UNTIL WE LOSE OUR FREEDOM, WE DON'T ALWAYS REALIZE HOW MUCH WE SHOULD TREASURE IT.

Freedom is one of the most precious things we possess. Yet until we lose it, we don't always realize how much we should treasure it.

I can't stand the thought of being in tight spaces now. I hate that out-of-control feeling where all appears hopeless, even for a short time. The hyper-awareness brought on by my MRI may have increased my restriction repulsion.

Or maybe it stemmed from seeing the slave castle, a place I will never forget.

TEARS SHED AT ELMINA CASTLE

On our last trip to Africa, Carlos and I visited our churches and school for children, and also toured Elmina Castle.[4] In 1482, European traders turned a timber and gold marketplace into a Trans-Atlantic slave trade route. They built the slave castle on the Gold Coast of West Africa, now known as Ghana.

As we approached the looming castle, the tour guide told us of its tortuous history. Newly enslaved human beings were branded with a final memory of their homeland, before they were forever taken away. Those memories would not have been happy.

Any laughter stopped as we entered the poorly ventilated and dark dungeons. "Over 1,000 males and 500 female slaves were crowded into these quarters," the tour guide said.

I shivered. The stench of mold, mildew, and mounds of evaporated human waste and sickness painted a vivid picture. We walked through the haunted halls, where screams of terror and sorrowful cries seemed etched into the walls.

Our footsteps echoed behind us. I huddled closer to Carlos, as we walked and reflected on a life no man or woman should ever endure.

The guide said, "The men and women were divided, and the females were violated on a constant basis. A little known fact is how slave traders starved the African inhabitants. They wanted them to fit through a tiny passage as they boarded them on boats and sent them to the new world."

I shuddered as my eyes and mind tried to process this evidence of enslavement. My ears hurt from hearing the real and raw depictions of humans treated worse than animals. Through the voice of the tour guide, it felt as if the memories were alive. I too felt trapped in the brick and mortar of this horrid place, as the ghosts

---

4. http://elminacastle.info

of slaves came alive in my heart. I pulled back from the group and found a corner to hide in.

I bowed my head as tears streamed down my face, plopping on to the dusty cobble of the castle floor. I squeezed my eyes shut. I imagined the guttural howls of the oppressed women who had passed over the spot where I stood.

A vision swam before my closed eyes. I saw a stunning dark face, with innocent brown eyes. Fear carved over her flawless features. With her back forced against icy stone, I could see a filthy, swampy-smelling, hateful-looking man sneer upon approach. I couldn't help wondering how she felt as she huddled with no way to escape.

Could she have praised God through torment after torment? What did she feel?

How did she survive the mental agony of losing her home and the comfortable environment she had known? What about losing the people she had confided in, those she felt safe being herself with?

Did she look to the heavens for help? Did she wonder where her God was? Or did she know Him at all? Did she realize that her Father in heaven wept over her pain, because her misery was not part of His plan? Did she know the sin of her captors was not her fault?

In the corridor of that castle, my compassion spread in a pool at my feet. If I could have spoken to this beautiful woman and countless others like her, I knew what I would have said: God sees you, and He loves you. He has not abandoned you. Not only does He see your pain, but He feels it, too. He cries with you.

YOUR CONCERNS ARE GOD'S CONCERNS

For those who want to begin again, but feel bound by circumstance, loss, or emotional imprisonment, I want to speak to your confinement. Because God is concerned about what concerns you. Your failed relationship matters to your Maker.

+ God sees your heart concerning the wrong decision trapping you in spiritual captivity.

+ Jesus cares about your unfulfilling job.

+ The Holy Spirit wants to help you move past that emotional injury you can't seem to let go of.

+ Jesus understands your insecurity, lack of confidence, and discouragement.

+ God knows the inner fears that tell you that your children's poor decisions are all your fault.

+ The Holy Spirit wants you to release the thoughts binding up your joy.

Bondage comes in many forms. But we are not like the slave woman, who could see no hope for a way out. We have Jesus.

JESUS OFFERS A WAY OUT

Jesus offered the ultimate sacrifice so we could live in freedom. However, too many of us huddle in a corner, staring at the dungeon door that's swung wide open. We are unwilling to believe it's as easy as accepting His grace so we can stroll on out.

Instead, we allow our past failures to bind us in our present place. We let habitual thoughts, doubts, and fears rob us of freedom. We listen to toxic people who convince us we don't deserve another chance. We falsely believe our former submissions to temptation require ongoing incarceration. So we surrender to them again and again, in a pattern of giving up over and over. We fall into deception, convinced that the sins perpetuated against us must somehow be our fault.

And through it all, we beat ourselves up with thoughts of regret. We cower under a gray cloud that darkens our minds, persuading us that we don't deserve God's gifts of mercy and grace.

The truth is, we don't.

Because of His grace, He gives us the very thing we don't deserve, and His mercy holds back what we should receive. Lovingly, He does not force His gifts into our hands—it's up to us to open our hands and receive them. So we can begin again.

It's time to step out of the shackles of imprisonment holding us back. It's time to let go of the warden mentality perpetuating self-bondage. We must turn the key and free ourselves from ongoing, self-induced captivity. It's time to walk away, free from thoughts that say, I don't want to get burned or embarrassed again. I've never done this before. How do I know this won't backfire? What if I fail?

Maybe you're enslaved by a martyr mentality. Your thoughts may sound like this: I don't want people to think I'm happy. I can't draw attention to myself—what if someone thinks I think too highly of myself? I don't want to lose my family and friends. They might treat me differently if I go for it. What if I succeed?

I'm sure I'm not the only one who has thought this way. But this kind of thinking gets us into trouble.

TORMENTED MAN LIVED IN A GRAVEYARD

Too many people refuse to begin again because they are listening to the wrong voices. This happened to a young man who literally lived in a graveyard.

Luke 8:26–40 tells the story of Jesus and His disciples traveling across the Sea of Galilee to the country of the Gadarenes, where they were met by a naked man who was tormented by demons. This man lived in a graveyard and although he was able to break free of chains and shackles, he was definitely stuck in his circumstance. Mark 5:5 says the poor guy was always crying and cutting himself with stones.

When the man saw Jesus, instead of running away, he ran to Him and fell down before Him. Jesus commanded the demons to leave the man. He permitted them to enter a herd of pigs, which promptly ran down a cliff and drowned in a lake.

The herdsmen who saw all of this were blown away. They fled to a nearby town and surrounding countryside to tell people the news. I'd say the gossip train had left the station.

By the time the crowd gathered to see this sight for themselves, the formerly tormented man had put on some clothes and was calmly sitting at Jesus's feet. But instead of celebrating with him, the people allowed a great fear to sweep over them and begged Jesus to go away.

Isn't that how some people react to someone else's good news? "I don't know what happened to you and I don't care. Go away and leave me alone. I don't have time for you."

The man who was healed of demons was so grateful, he wanted to join Jesus as one of His followers. But Jesus had a bigger idea, saying, *"Go home to your own people and tell them how much the Lord has done for you, and how he has had mercy on you"* (Mark 5:19).

The Bible tells us the man did exactly that. He went through Decapolis, proclaiming all the great things Jesus had done for him.

For a deeper understanding, you need to know a little detail: Decapolis wasn't a single town—it was ten major cities. So as this man shared his story, he became an evangelist, sharing the good news with many people. *"And all the people were amazed"* (Mark 5:20). After he was healed, God was still writing this man's story. His testimony started a new chapter.

God has a new chapter for you, too. He's got great things in store for you. Your breakthrough is just around the corner. Get ready to share your own good news.

> EVEN AFTER WE'VE RECEIVED OUR ULTIMATE HEALING, GOD'S NOT FINISHED WITH US.

Even after we've received our ultimate healing, God's not finished with us. The deeper our pain, the more dramatic our situation, and the longer it continues—all can mean a greater reach. A bigger story can equate to a larger number of people we encourage. Our ability to share what God has done is part of the continuing story He is writing in our lives.

To be free means you are released—unconfined, unbound, untied, unchained, and unshackled. Jesus sets us free from the self-imposed bondage that makes us shuffle through the tombs of past sin. We don't have to stumble up and down hills of recurring thoughts. Friends, we need to stop listening to the opinions of people who do not matter. God is the one we should strive to please.

Cut off your padlocks of regret and anger. And for crying out loud, don't step out of the graveyard only to run back again. When the Son sets you free, you are free indeed. Your past is not the problem; it's only when you live there that you're stuck. Keep in mind, if we don't encounter our pain, many of us would not encounter Jesus.

Even if you feel like your life is best represented by a cemetery, do not doubt that God has a vision and dream for you. When we accept Christ's gifts of grace and mercy, the process of our release begins. When the Spirit of the Lord resides in us, we are released into an unimpeded, unobstructed, and unrestricted life. We are set free. It's here that God continues to write our stories, greater than anything we imagined.

> YOUR PAST IS NOT THE PROBLEM;
> IT'S ONLY WHEN YOU LIVE THERE THAT YOU'RE STUCK.

HIKER WAS LITERALLY STUCK

Just like He did for Aron Lee Ralston[5]. April 26, 2003, was a fairly typical hiking day for Aron, as he made his way through Blue John Canyon in eastern Wayne County, Utah. But in a moment, his lighthearted journey took a heavy turn.

While he descended into a slot canyon, a boulder dislodged. The enormous rock smashed his left hand and then crushed his right into the canyon wall. Aron was stuck in a bad situation. He had not informed anyone of his hiking route, nor did he have a way to call for help.

Pinned against solid rock, he spent five agonizing days sipping on a small amount of water and nibbling his remaining food. He frantically tried to free his arm from the 800-pound boulder. After three days of failed attempts to lift or break it, a dehydrated and delirious Aron prepared to amputate his trapped right arm.

He carved his name, date of birth, and presumed date of death into the sandstone canyon wall, then videotaped final goodbyes to his family, not expecting to survive the night.

After waking at dawn the following morning, Aron had an epiphany. He realized he could use torque pressure against his trapped forearm to break the bones. Within an hour, he accomplished his goal.

Weak from shock, hunger, and dehydration, Aron climbed out of his slot canyon prison. He rappelled down a sixty-five-foot sheer wall, then hiked out. He was eight miles from his vehicle and had no phone. But he encountered a family who gave him food and water. They alerted the authorities, and saved his life.

---

5. https://www.aronralstonspeaker.com

Later, Aron Ralston spoke of his fears and the power of release. He knew that amputation was the only way that he would win his freedom from the canyon. He had to let go to fully live—to gain, he had to sacrifice.

Aron's story is a dramatic representation of release. But it provides us with a formula for letting go of the things that are pinning us against a wall, the circumstances and situations keeping us from beginning again.

BEGINNING AGAIN MAY MEAN LETTING GO

What are you holding on to? Sometimes, beginning again means cutting something out of your life. It requires a disconnect from anything that hinders God's plan for you.

Are you ready to begin again? What are you willing to cut out of your life that's keeping you stuck?

You were not born for the burden of a slavery yoke. Ephesians 3:12 assures us that because of Christ and our faith in Him, we can boldly approach God with freedom and confidence. But to receive, we must first release.

> ACCESS GOD'S PROMISE AS HIS BELOVED
> AND WELCOMED CHILD.

Free yourself, through the power of Jesus Christ, to experience the fullness of your story, the one God wants to write on your life. Accept His grace and mercy, allowing you to overcome any struggle. Access God's promise as His beloved and welcomed child. You already have your freedom and you don't have to cut off an arm to walk in it. All you need is a simple decision of faith.

When things appear hopeless, what would happen if you consulted God and listened for the guidance of His Holy Spirit?

What if you allowed yourself to aspire, desire, wish, expect, dream, design, and plan?

If you've dared to hope before, and felt the sting of hurt in the past, please realize that Jesus is the king of fresh starts. With Him in your corner, you can and should dare to begin again.

There may be times when we need to move something out of our way before we can make forward progress. We need to free up time, resources, and especially energy before our hopes transform into reality. But if you feel stuck and unable to get moving, I've got good news. In the coming chapters, we're going to look at some areas that often trip us up—or worse, keep us stuck. Whatever is going on, don't stop hoping. Instead, dare to begin again.

I D.A.R.E. YOU TO RELEASE

Decide: Release the emotional, mental, and spiritual chains that bind you. Jesus has already unlocked the door; it's up to you to walk through it.

Allow: Let God use your story to encourage others. Tell what He has done in you, for you, and through you as a result of your release.

Rise: What are you holding on to? Rise beyond your fears. Stand up to your demons and your naysayers, and dare to follow the script God is writing for your life.

Enjoy: Celebrate your freedom in faith. You don't need to keep revisiting your prison cell. The Son has set you free, so you are free indeed.

Chapter 4

HOPE AGAIN

Hope is one of those invisible essentials. You can't see it, touch it, taste it, or smell it, but you can definitely feel it. If you don't have hope, life loses all meaning. Hope is more than the pretty icing on the cake of life—it's that blend of secret ingredients making us rise and giving us flavor. Personally, I like mine a little sweet.

When I looked up synonyms of hope in my thesaurus, various words came up: aspiration, desire, wish, expectation, ambition, goal, dream, design, and plan, to name a few. But I wonder if you've had any experiences like mine, where you hope, dream, and plan, only to have life take you in an unexpected direction. I was in the middle of my sixth grade year when this very thing happened, in a most interesting way.

My class was studying dinosaurs and we even took a trip to the Smithsonian Institution in Washington, D.C. You could smell the history as soon as you walked inside. Our footsteps echoed through the glossy corridor, adding to my sense of reverence. For an eleven-year-old kid, it felt like walking on holy ground. And then we entered the holy of holies, the dinosaur exhibit.

I stretched my neck to take in the full height of the giant frames of a Tyrannosaurus rex and wooly mammoth. I couldn't absorb enough detail. Those tusks, those massive teeth, femurs as big as trees—I had never been more intrigued or amazed about an animal. I stood spellbound for hours, inching my way around their displays, so I could take in every angle.

When we boarded the bus for home a few hours later, my imagination raced as I kept thinking about one thing the tour guide had said: "Some of the most valuable dinosaur bones have been discovered on farmland." The reason for my excitement? I had access to a farm.

I grew up in somewhat of a mega-ministry. My dad and mom, Victor and Carmen Torres, founded New Life For Youth. Previously, Dad ran the streets as a gang member, until David Wilkerson of *The Cross and the Switchblade* fame inspired him to turn his life over to Jesus.

Today, people from all walks of life benefit from our programs. Pain knows no position or bank account balance.

> PAIN KNOWS NO POSITION OR BANK ACCOUNT BALANCE.

These precious people have histories filled with drugs, crime, abuse, and other traumatic issues. But they find hope and learn how to experience new life through our ministry. We focus on discipline, order, and other practical applications through our teaching methods, especially on the ranch.

God blessed our ministry with a special piece of property, a 118-acre farm dedicated to young men who know tough stuff. They learn the hard work of hoeing, weeding, watering, harvesting, and preparing food from the ground, and it helps them process their emotions in a physical way. The work gives them a sense of accomplishment and the satisfaction of a seeing a job completed. Many have never known the pleasure that comes from literally enjoying the fruits of their labor.

It's great therapy. And the farm was a great place for me to grow up around.

During the summers of my youth, I was like one of the guys, in a protected kind of way. Wherever they went, I went. Our beautiful ranch provided lots of space for adventure and exploration.

When I was in sixth grade, another staff member's kid and I were around the same age and good friends. In that season of our lives, we had a lot in common, including a burning desire to discover something great. After my trip to the Smithsonian, with hope in our hearts, we decided this was it. We were going to discover something great: dinosaur bones. We convinced ourselves this was our time.

So off we went on our great quest, with burlap bags in our hands. We packed sandwiches and some water, then headed off on our big adventure to hunt dinosaur bones.

A couple of hours later, with light films of sweat and grime painting our young faces, we stopped mid-step. Almost simultaneously. We looked at each other, first with open mouths, then with slowly spreading smiles. This. Was. It!

Both of us sprinted to the mound.

Hope pulsed with every pound of my heart. I couldn't believe it. Something white protruded out of the ground, glistening under the mid-day sun. I grinned at my friend. "I can't believe it. We did it. We found dinosaur bones."

Excitement bubbled in my belly as we began to dig. It felt like we would never get to the base of the bone. But eventually, we were able to pull out the largest rib I'd ever seen in my life.

We gasped with excitement. Could this really be what we thought it was?

I knew from my visit to the Smithsonian that a find like this was rare. We spent the rest of the afternoon feverishly digging out

more ribs. One by one, we laid them on the ground in careful for-
mation. When we plucked the last piece from the soil, we stepped
back to survey the big picture.

No doubt about it, we were looking at the remains of an
ancient dinosaur.

"I can't wait to call the Smithsonian and tell them what we've
found," I said.

"How much do you think it's worth?" my friend asked.

I hadn't considered money. I knew from overhearing Dad and
Mom talk that supporting a ministry was challenging. The only
outside aid we got came from occasional donations and miracles
from God. A new tremor of hope filled my gut. Maybe our dinosaur bones could end up being one of those miracles.

"I'm not sure. But I pray it's a lot," I said. "I can't wait to call the
Smithsonian and let them know what we found."

We made a pact to keep our discovery top secret. "No telling any adults at the ranch." We would not even tell our families.
At least not yet. We didn't want anyone taking all the money we
would receive. I couldn't believe we were going to become rich and
famous.

For a moment, I allowed myself to imagine what it would feel
like to walk up to my parents with a stack of cash. I envisioned the
tears in their eyes as I placed the green bills in their hands. I wiped
a tear off the edge of my cheek.

Before leaving the field, we carefully dragged all the bones
out of sight, and covered them with branches and leaves. Then we
flagged our find and raced back to the farm. We had lots to do
before the big news broke.

I ran into the house and scanned my dad's bookshelves. There
it was. I pulled down a copy of the encyclopedia. I needed to verify
our findings, like any good explorer.

My friend and I looked at the picture next to dinosaur fossils, scanning for similarities. Exact match.

We grabbed each other's shoulders, jumped up and down, and tried to keep our voices down, but it was hard not to squeal. "We did it, we did it," we giggled and whispered to each other.

All of a sudden, one of the adult leaders entered the room. "What are you guys up to?"

"Nothing," we looked at each other and snickered.

"Looks like a lot more than nothing to me. Come on, give. What's going on?"

We crumpled under the pressure like a line-dried sheet thrown into a laundry basket. We told him about the Smithsonian, our quest, and our discovery. Then we showed him the proof from the encyclopedia.

His face gave away his thoughts. He didn't have to say it out loud. I knew he was thinking, "You kids are crazy."

There was only one thing to do. We convinced him to go with us back to our hidden stash. He watched in silence while we pulled the tree branches back and methodically arranged the bones. We'd show him how foolish his skepticism was. Suddenly, we knew we had his attention.

He started laughing so hard his face turned red. I'm sure mine did, too, but not from laughter. What is his problem—can't he see we've discovered an entire dinosaur skeleton? He won't be laughing when the Smithsonian hands us the cash.

His laughter finally simmered down to periodic chuckles. A look of compassion spread over his features. He patted my friend's shoulder, then brushed the grungy light brown bangs out of my sweat-stung eyes. He said, "I'm sorry, kiddos, you dug up the cow we likely killed a year ago and ate for dinner."

Then the laughter grabbed his gut again. With each of his cackles, my dreams, plans, and hopes shriveled up and died.

> ## SOMETIMES, SHATTERED HOPE HITS YOU BETWEEN THE EYES.

Sometimes, shattered hope hits you between the eyes, and for those in the target area, it's no laughing matter. When hope dies, people grieve—many for a lifetime, some while trusting for a miracle. And some look a little crazy for hoping at all.

DANIEL KNEW WHERE TO PLACE HIS HOPE

I'm sure there were people who thought Daniel was nuts for daring to hope, especially when the king locked him up with a pack of hungry lions. But Daniel was wise—he knew where to place his hope. We can hope for a lot of things, but not all are wise. I don't know about you, but I've made that mistake before, too many times.

In Daniel chapter six, he is the king's most distinguished and trusted servant, positioned over the entire kingdom. This infuriated some other guys who were in leadership positions. They were so jealous, they decided to try to dig up some dirt about Daniel. Jealousy can do some crazy things to the human mind. But Daniel was a man of integrity, so although his enemies looked hard, they could find no reason to accuse him of wrong-doing.

That's another lesson we can learn from Daniel. There were no signs of corruption or negligence in his personnel file. He lived in a trustworthy manner.

So the jealous dudes shifted their plan and moved on to flattery. They stroked the king's ego and manipulated him into issuing a decree that for thirty days, everyone could only pray to the king. Don't you just hate weasels? But the kicker was the punishment.

Anyone who disobeyed this new law would be thrown into a den of hungry lions.

This created a real dilemma for Daniel. As a man of committed faithfulness to the one and only true God, his integrity would not allow him to worship anything or anyone else. The Bible tells us in Daniel 6:10 that he knelt in prayer and thanksgiving to God three times a day.

The jealous men spied on Daniel and caught him praying to God, so they ran to the king to tattle on him. Know anyone like that? These guys accused Daniel of disrespecting the king by praying to his God instead of the king. The king was in a tough spot, too. They tricked him into signing the law and he couldn't change it without jeopardizing his position.

Daniel had to go into the lions' den. Worse, a big stone was placed over the entrance so he had no chance of escape.

But the bad guys had put their hope in the wrong thing, while Daniel put his hope in God. The king told Daniel, *"May your God, whom you serve continually, rescue you!"* (Daniel 6:16).

After an anxiety-filled night without sleep or food, the king rushed to the mouth of the lions' den and cried out, *"Daniel, servant of the living God, has your God, whom you serve continually, been able to rescue you from the lions?"* (Daniel 6:20).

You can imagine the king's relief when Daniel replied, *"My God sent his angel, and he shut the mouths of the lions. They have not hurt me, because I was found innocent in his sight"* (Daniel 6:22).

When the story concludes, the power of Daniel's well-placed hope is seen. God is honored, not just by Daniel, but also by the king and all his people, through a new edict. And the jealous guys who perpetrated the plot paid the ultimate price for their deceit— as lion fodder themselves.

As a dinosaur-hunting kid, I had a different source of hope than Daniel. I meant well, but I hadn't discussed my hope placement with the one and only true God. Daniel did.

Disillusionment could have caused me to give up, like a lot of people I've met. Especially in my field of work, you meet a lot of hopeless people.

A few years back, something unusual happened to me and my husband that showed me the influence of hope.

HURTING PEOPLE LEARN TO HOPE IN THE LORD

In an exercise meant to spur healing for wounded people, we were asked to stand in front of a room and represent proxy parents to people in the audience. Then everyone else was invited to come forward and speak to us as if we were their parents. Adult after adult rose and stepped toward us.

A gorgeous woman with stylish red hair, sassy clothes, and accessories to spare walked up to me. She said, "Mom, how could you let that man do that to me?"

I admit her words stunned me.

Another lady approached. She had a gentle face, a shy smile, and a tender demeanor. She whispered, "Mom, why couldn't you love me for me?"

A third woman came to me. "Mom, where were you when I needed you?"

A fourth said, "Mom, why didn't you show me how to deal with conflict so I don't hurt people in the process?"

Another said, "Mom, why haven't I ever been good enough?"

A guy came forward, "Mom, why didn't you teach me how to cope with failure?"

The next one said, "Mom, how come you wouldn't hug me?"

The next time I looked up, I was startled. A man stepped all up in my space. With tears streaming off his chin, he said, "Mom, why did you let your boyfriend rape me? I was just a little boy."

That did it. I sobbed under the weight of their wounds. But the healing part was still to come.

> GOD IS YOUR PERFECT PARENT AND HE LOVES YOU NO MATTER WHAT.

Once every willing person had courageously expressed their hurt, disappointment, and anger, the speaker brought it home. He reminded the wounded that their hope was in the Lord. He told the audience, "God is your perfect parent and He loves you no matter what. He won't reject you. He won't ignore you. He won't turn His back on what's happened to you. He won't abandon you. He's waiting for you to bring it all to Him, as many times as you want. He won't get tired of listening." That's inspired hope.

WHAT KEEPS YOU FROM HOPE?

So as I write, I wonder, *What keeps you from daring to hope?*

+ Are you afraid someone will laugh at you? Even if they do, is that the worst thing that could happen today?

+ Are you afraid you're going to make a mistake? So what if you do? We're not God—we can't get it right all the time. But if we never try, we're sure to fail.

+ Are you afraid of what someone else might do to you? Take your concerns to God. He has a plan, a place, or a person aligned to help you. He's still in the miracle-making business.

What if your fear of hope causes you to miss out on the story He still wants to write on your life? What if He has something special intended for you, and your refusal means the gift goes to someone else?

You don't have to worry. It's not too late. God's still in the restoration business.

In the next chapter, we'll explore one of the hardest, most crucial aspects to helping us begin again. Daring to forgive will propel you farther than you can imagine. It's the ink in the pen of God's promise—and He's offering it to you.

I D.A.R.E. YOU TO HOPE

Decide: You can resolve to hope before you feel it. If you've buried your hope, decide to unearth it—the feelings will come after action.

Allow: God's going to use someone, so why not let it be you? Accept the gifts, talents, abilities, and opportunities He puts in front of you.

Rise: Reclaim your hope and let it rise up in you. Don't crush it; don't run from it; don't hide it away.

Enjoy: Hope-filled people are happy people. Give yourself permission to have the happiness you say you want.

Chapter 5

FORGIVE AGAIN

Forgiveness is one of those topics that have been written, spoken, and sung about for millennia. At some point in their lives, almost every human being who has ever sucked air into their lungs wrestles with forgiveness. We either fight the idea of forgiving someone else or, sometimes harder, forgiving ourselves.

But what does it mean to forgive? Some of the definitions I found say it means to stop feeling angry or resentful toward someone for an offense, flaw, or mistake. It's defined as canceling a debt. One says it excuses or regards indulgently another person's shortcomings, ignorance, or impoliteness. That's fancy talk for not givin' a jerk what they deserve.

As a mom, one of the hardest things I've had to forgive is the hurt someone caused one of my three babies. No matter how busy I am or how much ministry work there is to do, my husband and children come first after God. And there'd best be no one messing with my family, or they will have this Latina fireball to contend with. Remember those lions in Daniel's den? Grrrr!

Among my three kids, I only have one daughter, Alana. As you can imagine, she's our princess and has always been mama's special girl.

When she was little, I dressed her up like a doll. I made sure she had a matching bow or hat, coordinated with her frilly socks. With her long, curly hair and eyes that sparkled, she was my everything. She did well in school and enjoyed her playmates with few problems...until third grade.

MEAN GIRLS' WORDS CAN DAMAGE TENDER HEARTS.

That's when the bullying began. You've likely heard the term "mean girls," but I'm telling you, the girls in Alana's class got downright dirty. Girls can say the most horrible words and with them, they wield the power to damage a tender heart's self-worth, self-esteem, and confidence.

By fifth grade, Alana's grades began to slip and I noticed she would say things like, "Mommy, I can't do this. I'm scared. What if I fail?"

I had a hard time understanding where this language came from. We had lifted her up since the day she was born.

It especially confused me since she doesn't come from a heritage of shrinking violets. We're more like big, bold, in-your-face sunflowers.

I wanted my sunflower back. I wanted her to blossom and shine like the beautiful, bold girl God made her to be. So I began to work on her confidence. Every day, I made her repeat back to me, "I can do all things through Christ who strengthens me." Over and over, she said it. And little by little, my Alana began to believe the words she spoke.

There were times during her teenage years when Alana still struggled. You either have a teenager, were a teenager, or are one now, so you know what I mean, especially when faced with persistent bullies. But as Alana chose to act with courage and leaned into Christ's strength, she began to grow. Her petals were unfolding.

> ## I CAN DO ALL THINGS THROUGH CHRIST WHO STRENGTHENS ME.

After her high school graduation, we received word of a huge financial blessing. God had opened the door to a college she hoped to attend through a singing scholarship.

When we arrived for orientation, Alana and I clutched each other's arms in the thrill of the moment. She was here, God had made a way. But just as quickly as Alana's enthusiasm had fired up, it fizzled out. Her old insecurities reared their ugly heads.

"Mom, what if I can't do this? What if all the things the kids in school said about me are true?" Both of our smiles faded.

Tears welled in my eyes before I said, "Baby, you are too smart to believe those kinds of lies."

But sadly, I could tell the years of messages delivered by bullies were replaying in her mind. Deflated? I felt flatter than a balloon with no air.

My baby girl expressed her frustration. "This was going to be my fresh start. Why can't I just put the past behind me?"

I grabbed Alana's face, pulled her near, looked directly into her eyes, and encouraged her. "Don't give up—we've come too far. God's opened this door for you. Don't you dare give in to defeat. Refuse the temptation to quit. Pick up the pieces and begin again."

I knew she still had fear in her heart, but Alana received my admonition and from that moment forward, she bravely placed her faith over her feelings. Time went by, and during one phone call, Alana happily reported her excitement over all of the new friends she had made. It seemed she was finally free of the grief from her past.

Until one day on a singing tour in New York. Alana was asked to go on the trip because of a senior's scheduling conflict. But right before their first production, Alana's leader informed her they didn't need her to sing after all. The senior ended up rearranging her schedule so she could make the engagement. Alana called me, discouraged.

"Why did God have me come on this trip when I have so much homework to catch up on? If I'm not going to sing, I need to be back on campus. This doesn't make sense."

> SOMETIMES, GOD WANTS US TO SIT
> AND WAIT FOR HIM TO REVEAL HIS PLANS.

I reminded her that sometimes, God wants us to sit and wait for Him to reveal His plans.

When she called me the next night, her entire perspective had changed. "Mom, you aren't going to believe what happened."

"What?" I said, imagining what she might have to say. I couldn't guess.

"One of the girls who used to give me a hard time in school? She's here. In New York."

My mama bear fur bristled.

Alana continued. "After the production, she walked up to me, and I recognized her immediately. I felt like I was going to throw up."

"I'll bet, baby. I'm sorry." I braced myself. "What kind of mean things did she say this time?"

"No, you don't understand. She came right to me and said, 'Will you forgive me? I feel so bad about the way I treated you all those years.'" Alana laughed, in lighter spirits than I'd heard in some time. "Mom, she asked me to forgive her. So I did. On the spot. I feel so much better now. And actually, it's made me realize I need to reach out to some people I might have hurt and ask them to forgive me. I'm going to make some calls and invite a few people to coffee as soon as I get back. Isn't that great?"

"That is great," I agreed. Truth be told, if she had said anything different, the mama bear in me would have definitely risen up.

Alana stayed true to her decision and made those calls. One girl in particular agreed to make immediate plans for coffee with my daughter.

As they talked, Alana poured out her pain from the things that had happened in their shared past. To her surprise, Alana found out the girl had no idea how she felt.

Alana ended up offering the girl forgiveness and grace, and asking for the same in return. Both of them praised God as they parted ways, experiencing both release and relief. They're friends today.

In each conversation with her former antagonists, my daughter was unshackled from her past pain. Each time she asked someone to forgive her for the offenses she might have caused, God set Alana free to begin again. And He's still writing her story.

But Mama got a lesson, too. It's one thing to talk forgiveness, but it's a whole other thing to walk it. Do you get me?

> IT'S ONE THING TO TALK FORGIVENESS, BUT IT'S A WHOLE OTHER THING TO WALK IT.

When considering all the amazing stories of healing powered by forgiveness in the Bible, one in particular strikes my heart. Joseph knew bullying. But so much like my Alana, his daring move to forgive unlocked the shackles of his emotional prison, too.

GOD PLANTED DREAMS IN JOSEPH'S HEART

As is the case so often, Joseph was young when the bullying began. In that season of innocence, he dared much. He dared to dream and he dared to hope. Bullies are afraid of those who dare.

It wasn't Joseph's fault God gave him dreams. They were gifts planted in his heart, mind, and spirit from the time he was born. But they didn't sprout and flourish until he was seventeen years old. His older brothers, however, did not like the promises God spoke to Joseph through his dreams, so they conspired against him. (See Genesis 37:5–11.)

Hate is a deadly thing.

In verse 18, things heat up. Some of Joseph's siblings wanted to kill him, but his brother Reuben came up with an alternative plan. He suggested they throw him into a dry cistern instead, so they did. You think you have family problems? Can you imagine your family having this conversation about you—do we keep him or do we kill him? Reuben's real motive was to come back and rescue Joseph later on. But something happened that changed everything.

Some traveling merchants were passing by and another brother came up with a new plot. To paraphrase Genesis 37:26–27, Judah said, "Let's sell him to the Ishmaelites. We won't have his blood on our hands and we'll make some money."

Can we get real? This kind of behavior ticks me off. Yet it's no surprise for bullies to act this way.

> BULLIES EXIST IN A BUBBLE OF FEAR AND JEALOUSY, SCARED SOMEONE ELSE MIGHT SUCCEED AND THEY WON'T.

Bullies exist in a bubble of fear and jealousy, scared someone else might succeed and they won't. They spend their energy tearing people down, rather than looking for ways to build others up. They aren't focused on a positive purpose for their own lives. This makes me wonder how many bullies miss out on the good gifts God wants to give them. By reacting out of their emotions, their fear of lack often becomes reality.

The Bible shows us in detail how Joseph's brothers bullied him. But as I read in Genesis, I'm especially struck by Joseph's ability to stay calm and carry on while God wrote his story. Repeatedly, Joseph dared to forgive again so God could free him to begin again. Three things particularly stand out to me.

+ Joseph did not dwell on the past; he spent his time and energy focused on the moment and the task in front of him.

+ Joseph did not justify responsive behaviors by lashing out in attempts to make others pay.

+ Joseph did not waste his efforts playing God by trying to control people or situations.

Based on what I've read about Joseph's life, he had to make the decision to forgive over and over. Throughout his life, he endured multiple offenses from a myriad of people. But I see no evidence of his complaining or whining. I imagine he practiced forgiveness skills because human instinct does not tell us to offer others the grace and mercy Jesus extends to us. Yet, in God's Word, we are told to offer exactly that.

I'm still practicing. In some instances, I do well, while in others, I fail. I'm going to speak the truth here: I'm a work in progress. What about you?

If there's anything Joseph's biblical account proves, it's that deciding to forgive again, over and over, is worth it. When God wrote "The End" on Joseph's life, it was a beautiful, peace-filled resolution. Joseph was honored for his grace-filled living, not just by his family and close friends, but in foreign lands among powerful people.

Thankfully, Joseph followed the script God was writing for his life; otherwise, the ultimate outcome might not have turned out so well, not only for Joseph and his family, but for yours and mine as well.

During his time on Earth, Joseph saved thousands of lives by listening to God and obeying him. Because he did, there's a good chance one of our ancestors survived. Think about it: Joseph's legacy still benefits us today. In the scope of millennia that's passed since Joseph lived, millions of people have migrated around the planet, and many came from Egypt. Some may have been your ancestors. We may have breath in our bodies today because Joseph dared to begin again.

I'm sure there were times Joseph didn't feel like forgiving someone who had wronged him, but he did it anyway. When life feels unfair and we wonder how God could ask us to forgive someone, especially when they don't deserve it—and who does, by the way?—we would do well to remember Joseph. He dared to forgive again and again, offering kindness and love to those who "thought evil" against him. God honored Joseph's obedience by writing many blessings into the rest of his life. Don't we all want to receive the promises God is willing to pen?

> JOSEPH DARED TO FORGIVE AGAIN AND AGAIN, OFFERING KINDNESS AND LOVE TO THOSE WHO "THOUGHT EVIL" AGAINST HIM.

These are the questions I want you to consider today:

What will the end of your story look like? Will you leave a legacy as a person who allowed God to work in you and through you, perhaps saving lives? Or will wasted years of wallowing in your wounds come with consequences that come at a high price for you and those around you?

What will you be known for? Will you leave behind a reputation of grace and mercy or one of anger and revenge?

Who have you struggled to forgive? A perpetrator of an abuse or crime? A parent? Someone you paid? A brother or sister? A co-worker? Or maybe, like my precious Alana, you struggle to forgive bullies, especially when you can't seem to get away from them.

For some of us, the person we struggle the most to forgive is the one we see in the mirror. However, God calls us to a life of forgiveness for all. This includes extending grace and mercy to ourselves.

Think about it: if God is willing to forgive us, but we refuse to forgive ourselves, what are we saying? That we know more than Him? Not cool—and this definitely puts a block on the story He wants to write for our lives.

The questions above may sting with conviction as you reflect on them—I told you I wasn't going to sugarcoat the truth—but remember, it's not too late. God's still writing your story, if you let Him. Daring to begin again starts with decisions and actions beyond your emotions. The truth is, no one who has offended, hurt, stolen, abused, wounded, or bullied deserves forgiveness. But somewhere in life, we all fall into one or more of these categories, whether we intended harm or not.

> THANKFULLY, GOD DOES NOT GIVE US WHAT WE DESERVE. HE GENEROUSLY GIVES US MERCY AND GRACE.

Thankfully, God does not give us what we deserve. He generously gives us mercy and grace. This is forgiveness in action—simple, but far from easy. If you want the end of your story to turn out well, dare to forgive again and don't sell yourself short. Dare to listen to the voice of the One who knows best, even when what He's asking doesn't seem to make sense.

I D.A.R.E. YOU TO FORGIVE

Decide: What are you holding on to that's blocking God's pen of promise for your life? Decide to forgive, even if you don't feel it, and trust Jesus to guide your emotions until they follow.

Allow: Let God write healing into the pain and past keeping you from the blessings He is waiting to provide. You free yourself when you forgive.

Rise: Refuse to give in to your feelings, the ones that tell you to lash out, fight to defend yourself, or to justify. Trust God who holds the pen. He's not done writing your story.

Enjoy: Give yourself permission to love life, regardless of old history. Dwell on what you have and celebrate with others when they succeed.

Chapter 6

LISTEN AGAIN

Have you ever been in a situation in which you wished you could have a do-over? Maybe it's a mess of your own making. Maybe a trusted friend tried to warn you, but you simply did not listen. Or perhaps you trusted the wrong person, and took the wrong advice. Whatever the circumstance, you've thought, *I wouldn't mind having a DeLorean right about now.*

I know you remember the great *Back to the Future* movie trilogy starring Michael J. Fox. I grew up with those movies. The music was great—I could sing along with Huey Lewis like nobody's business. I'll even admit I had a little crush on Mr. Fox, though he was a bit height challenged for me, since I was the tallest girl in my class.

In the original film, Dr. Emmett Brown, a crazy, wild-haired scientist with a sheepdog named Einstein, invented the flux capacitor. When this Y-shaped component was inserted into the DeLorean, Doc Brown said, "This is what makes time travel possible."

As I watched the movie, I wondered, Where would I go if I had a time machine available? Would I watch them put the Eiffel Tower's cap in place? Would I join Lewis and Clark as they discovered new territories? Would I meet up with Jesus, as He walked from Jerusalem to Nazareth?

What about you? What spot in history would you want to travel to if you had a flux capacitor? Where would you go? Who would you want to see? Imagine watching Thomas Edison sign the patent papers for the light bulb. Or passing a turkey leg to one of the early settlers at the first Thanksgiving. You could sit down for a fried banana and peanut butter sandwich with Elvis. Or play catch with a young Babe Ruth in a suburb of Baltimore.

How amazing would it be to sit in a boat while Peter strolled across the water toward Jesus? Or see the look on Mary's and Martha's faces when Lazarus rose from the dead?

As wonderful as it would be to view these historical events in person, it's our own history that most of us would like to revisit. Like Marty in *Back to the Future*, we'd prefer time travel that allows us to correct past and future wrongs. If you sat in the seat when that silver DeLorean with gull-wing doors hit eighty-eight miles per hour, where would you go?

In Bible numerology, the number eight represents regeneration and resurrection. I don't know if Robert Zemeckis had this in mind when he wrote and directed *Back to the Future*, but he hit on a deep human need when he used that number.

I think most of us would like to fix at least one thing in our past. The option to regenerate, replace, and reform our present reality is tempting. We would all like to jump in at pivotal, crossroad moments in our histories, with a chance at a do-over.

As you read this, are you cringing at the memory of some decision you made that may have seemed good at the time, but turned out to be devastating in some way?

Some pangs may be caused by something as simple as regretting that prom dress, that hair style, or those gorgeous high-heeled shoes that were impossible to walk in. Other regrets might include not making better grades in school or wishing you'd taken better care of your health. You might want a re-do for an opportunity you missed. Perhaps you made a bad financial decision or got into an unhealthy relationship. Maybe your memory hurts too much to speak of it because you believe you did something unthinkable or something unthinkable was done to you.

WE ALL HAVE MOMENTS WE WISH WE COULD DO OVER.

Whatever the mistake, misstep, trauma or trouble, we all have moments we wish we could do over. We say to ourselves, If only I had LISTENED!

While driving, have you ever turned to a passenger and asked, "Anything coming on your side?" before pulling out onto the road?

Most of us have had people who looked out for us on our blind side. Your passenger has a different perspective than you do sitting behind the wheel. They might see a car coming or a child on a bicycle. They might spot some other danger that you can't see from where you're sitting.

The Bible tells us there is wisdom in a multitude of counsel. (See Proverbs 15:22.) God has placed people in our lives to help us see things we may not recognize due to lack of experience or outlook. Our slanted view from past experience or impaired emotions may blind us or cloud our judgment. A parent, boss, friend, or even a foe can become blind-side buds, sent by God to help us sort things out.

If we're honest, most of us can say we would be in a little better situation if we had listened to people who tried to warn us. God can even use our enemies, people we don't trust, to guide us. So how do you know who to listen to?

I have a friend who says, "Your opinion matters to me right up until the point where it's different than God's." That's a lot of wisdom right there.

IF THE ADVICE YOU RECEIVE LINES UP WITH WHAT GOD SAYS IN THE BIBLE, CONSIDER IT.

Test the advice you're given, whether it's from a trusted friend, an enemy, or even a pastor. Pray about what they've said and then listen. If the advice you receive lines up with what God says in the Bible, consider it. If it doesn't contradict what you know of God's character from studying His Word, then the guidance is likely solid. But to test it, you must go to the Bible. Truth is always spoken there.

Too often, we listen but don't hear because we're too focused on our emotions. In other cases, we hear but don't listen because it isn't what we hoped would cross our ears.

You might be thinking, *Wait. Hearing and listening are the same thing.* But actually, they're not.

Hearing is one of the five senses. We learned that in elementary school. According to Merriam-Webster, hearing is "the process, function, or power of perceiving sound." It simply means your ears have picked up on a noise. Listening, while it may require hearing, takes the process a step further. Listening starts when your brain receives the nerve impulses from the sound and then deciphers them. Listening requires thoughtful attention and consideration, which then leads to understanding. Hearing is a passive occurrence; unless you are hearing-impaired, it's automatic. Listening, on the other hand, requires active participation. Essentially, listening means you are a *doer* of the Word and not a *hearer* only.

So, what now? You don't have a time machine and here you are dealing with consequences of your past choices. You're not even sure you can trust yourself to make better decisions in the future. You've made it this far in the book, so you already know I'm not going to leave you stuck here. And neither is God.

> WE'VE ALL MADE BAD CHOICES, BUT GOD WILL INTERVENE AND GET US BACK ON THE PATH OF OUR PURPOSES.

Yes, we've all made bad choices, but God will intervene and get us back on the path of our purposes. He's been doing that sort of thing for a very, VERY long time. Let's look at Jonah.

JONAH KNEW GOD WOULD SPARE HIS ENEMIES

Jonah was a prophet who lived north of Nazareth during the reign of Jeroboam II. The Israeli ruler had expanded the borders of his nation to its greatest reaches since King David and King Solomon. But the Assyrian Empire made constant threats.

There are two important facts to keep in mind regarding Jonah's story:

1. Nineveh, Assyria's greatest city, was nicknamed the City of Blood. The people were idolatrous, proud, and brutal. In their passion to overthrow the world and slaughter those who got in the way, they especially hated Israel. God wanted Jonah to warn them that they needed to change their evil ways.

2. Jonah knew that the Lord is *"a gracious and compassionate God, slow to anger and abounding in love"* (Jonah 4:2), so he also knew that if the Nineveh heeded His warning, God would spare them. That's the last thing this patriotic Israelite wanted.

Needless to say, what God was telling him to do made no sense to Jonah. Can you imagine what kind of thoughts went through his mind? *So, wait. You want me to risk my life for these horrible, violent, and godless people who hate my guts? You want me to tell the evildoers who slaughtered my people how to avoid slaughter themselves?*

Here's what stands out to me about the situation:

+ Jonah heard God, but because God's instruction did not fall in line with what Jonah thought was best, he didn't want to consider what he was hearing.

+ Jonah heard, but he did not listen. In fact, he ran in the opposite direction. Did he think he could hide from God? Yes, he did. He was wrong.

WE CAN'T RUN AWAY FROM GOD FOR LONG.

Jonah boarded a ship sailing for Tarshish, away from Nineveh. But we can't run away from God for long. As the vessel made its way across the sea, God sent a mighty wind to let Jonah know He wasn't joking. A violent storm kicked up, threatening to destroy the ship and everyone on it. The sailors were panicking, screaming, and praying to their gods. They threw cargo overboard to keep the ship from sinking.

And where was Jonah? In the middle of the storm brought on by his disobedience, Jonah was below deck fast asleep. Sometimes, when we want to run away from something we don't want to hear, it's easier to hibernate for a while.

The captain woke Jonah up. "How can you sleep at a time like this?" he asked. "Get up and pray to your God! Maybe He will pay attention to us and spare our lives." (See Jonah 1:6.)

When the captain and crew learned that Jonah was a Hebrew who worshipped the one true God of heaven and earth, and he admitted he had disobeyed God, everyone realized that Jonah's actions had caused the storm. They threw him into the sea.

When we don't listen to God, there are consequences. Our disobedience affects everyone around us. You think you're not hurting anyone else and that your choices are your business? Think again. The unsuspecting sailors didn't choose to run from God— that was Jonah's choice. But the crew endured the same storm

Jonah did. Disobedience costs us and those around us unnecessary pain, needless trials, and precious time.

WHEN WE DON'T LISTEN TO GOD, THERE ARE CONSEQUENCES.

Jonah's problem wasn't that he couldn't hear God. He was a prophet, so he heard God quite clearly. Sometimes, we hear Him, too. When wrestling with a decision, we sometimes feel that nudge of conviction or get a nagging whisper of doubt. Or we may get a strong sense that the situation does not align with what God says in the Bible. If we pay attention, we realize He is proving this is not what He wants. The problem arises when we fail to follow through.

In other situations, we may understand His plan and accept His purpose, but then try to do God's thing our own way. We are afraid that obeying God will cost us too much. What we fail to realize is what Jonah failed to realize: NOT obeying God costs so much more. But even so, God is faithful and will provide a way out when we confess and repent.

If we confess our sins, he is faithful and just and will forgive us our sins and purify us from all unrighteousness. (1 John 1:9)

In other words, God is willing to wipe the slate clean so He can continue writing our story.

The sea turned calm when Jonah was thrown overboard and a great fish, perhaps a whale, swallowed him whole. I know that sounds like another terrible consequence, but drowning would be worse. That fish was actually God's provision to keep Jonah alive for three days, and perhaps give him some time to think and pray. Sometimes God's way of escape is not what we expect. But when we listen, He will quiet the storm and give us a way out of the trouble, allowing us to get back on track. Paul reminds us:

No temptation has overtaken you except what is common to mankind. And God is faithful; he will not let you be tempted beyond what you can bear. But when you are tempted, he will also provide a way out so that you can endure it.

(1 Corinthians 10:13)

My mother and father learned this first-hand. They had an extensive speaking ministry in over thirty countries, including the United States. They came to Virginia to speak, but for some reason, those Virginia dates got canceled. Friends encouraged my parents to make Richmond their home. But my father, a Puerto Rican kid from the streets of Brooklyn, didn't think the beautiful town needed their help. He used to say, "They've got more churches than supermarkets."

He used a tree to prove his point.

Richmond grows an abundance of our state tree, the flowering dogwood. In early spring, the tree grows gorgeous white and pink blossoms in the shape of a cross. Dad would tell my mom, "Look, Carmen, this city doesn't need us, and they don't need my kind of ministry here. There's so much religion here that *crosses* are growing on trees."

But he soon learned things weren't quite as they appeared. They made the move in the early 1970s. It wasn't an easy adjustment. Living in an unfamiliar, racially divided town, not particularly welcoming to a Latino couple, wasn't ideal. It didn't help that my mother didn't speak English.

In the early days of their transition, Dad and Mom met a lot of opposition. Although my dad was—and is still—a man of great faith, he became discouraged. It seemed like, of all the places God could send them, this was an odd choice. My dad needed a little more convincing.

My dad got on his knees and prayed: If you want me to stay in the city, I need to hear your voice. Then he grabbed his Bible and went downtown to Grace Street.

The hippie culture had gone mainstream by the early seventies. Grace Street jammed with long hair, bell bottoms, peace signs, and all of the underground elements of "sex, drugs, and rock & roll." The smell of marijuana hung in the air and psychedelic music spilled out of the smoky nightclubs lining the streets.

Bruce Springsteen played the Back Door Club in Richmond before making it big. With the number of young people going in and out, you'd think the place was giving away free beer and peyote.

Across the street, the Lee Art Theatre screened porn films and featured burlesque dancing. Even Lum's, a diner serving popular chocolate milkshakes, had prostitutes hanging around. Close by, the Biograph Theatre, an art house/repertory cinema, held late-night shows starting just after the bars closed.

Standing in the middle of that scene, my dad took a bold step forward and started preaching. Before he knew it, a crowd gathered. He preached his heart out that day, sharing how God had raised him off of the streets of New York, saving him from a life of gang violence and drug addiction. As more and more people stopped to listen, he told them how Jesus had turned his life around. He told them hope was available to them right there on that very street.

One brave young man's hand went up in the air at my dad's invitation to receive God's love and a relationship with His Son. Then, one by one, others came forward to ask Jesus Christ to enter their lives and forgive their sins. Although I wasn't there that day, I was able to relive that powerful scene during the filming of the documentary *One More Life*.[6]

The work God started on that day is still going strong. Today, tens of thousands of people have a relationship with God because

6. https://www.victortorres.org/about

my parents dared to listen to the call of Jesus. Young men and women struggling with life-controlling issues like drugs and alcohol, sex trafficking, self-injury, and eating disorders, have found freedom through Christ. At New Life For Youth, via our programs for men, women, and single mothers, many have dared to begin again. All because a Mexican girl and a Puerto Rican boy dared to follow God. Anywhere. Even when it didn't make sense to them, even when it was scary. They dared to listen.

Imagine the difference in outcome if my parents had understood what God asked of them, but like Jonah, ran the other way. Countless wounded people might have missed out on an opportunity to begin again. Those who've suffered domestic violence, human trafficking, emotional abuse, and made mistakes but found freedom, might have been denied fresh starts. But because my parents heard God, listened, and dared to obey, these same people received job and life-skills training. Their children are growing up in happy, healthy homes, grateful for clean slates.

HOW IS YOUR LISTENING? DO YOU HEAR GOD'S VOICE?

So how is your listening? Do you hear God's voice? Do you identify His instruction for your life when you're praying and reading His Word? Do you recognize His truth, spoken through a trusted godly friend? Do you know Him well enough to spot bad advice? Or are you running from what God has told you because you are afraid of confronting the hard, right thing you know you should do?

It might seem easier to turn a deaf ear to God's voice now. But if you do, like Jonah, disobeying God can cost you everything. Eventually.

James 1:19 gives us some listening tips: *"Let every person be quick to hear, slow to speak, slow to anger."* Sure, it sounds easy, but in reality, it's quite a challenge. Carlos could tell some stories about me. Just trying to keep it real. Often, we do the opposite of what James suggests. We are slow to hear, quick to speak, and even quicker to flash with fury.

> OFTEN, WE ARE SLOW TO HEAR, QUICK TO SPEAK, AND EVEN QUICKER TO FLASH WITH FURY.

You have to work at becoming a great listener. Think of it this way: after spending enough time with them, you learn to recognize the voices of people you know. Get to know God more intimately through his Word, the Bible. Speak to Him in prayer. Accept wise counsel from other people who know Him. Learn to listen by spending time in His presence.

You can't listen without hearing and you can't hear while you're talking. So put a stop to gossiping, complaining, and negativity. Also remember, hearing is passive. Listening requires active participation. The better you get at it, the less likely you'll need a DeLorean or a crazy, wild-haired scientist to set things right.

Listening to God isn't the only thing that feels crazy, especially when our circumstances are uncontrollable and unjust. Life is often unfair—a subject we'll tackle in the next chapter.

I D.A.R.E. YOU TO LISTEN

Decide: Stop running! Trust in God's purpose and plan for your life. Acknowledge that He is good and His way is the best way, then choose to act on it.

Allow: Just like Jonah, God is calling you. Yes, *you!* Surrender your heart and your desires. Let God fill you with His purpose.

Rise: God knows how to make a special purpose possible for your life. He can make it happen. Run after Him, not away from Him, and He will lift you up.

Enjoy: Listen for the still, small voice of Jesus. He is calling you to a great adventure. You don't want to miss it. Lounge at His feet and soak in His plans for you.

Chapter 7

SACRIFICE AGAIN

Sacrifice requires strength, and sacrifice runs through the veins of my sweet mama. She has a gentle spirit, but my dad and I are not the only ones with Latin spice in our blood. My Latina sass is a natural by-product of my maternal heritage.

My mother grew up on beautiful farmland in the hills of Mexico. Young Carmen was surrounded by family, goats, chickens, and other animals. As she describes it, she enjoyed a simple, joy-filled life.

When Mom was a young girl, her light brown hair and green-hued hazel eyes gained her a lot of attention, especially when she blossomed into her teens. And she was as talented as she was beautiful. Clothed in dresses made by her own hand, she was crowned the Queen of Soccer in her town. She was also blessed with an hourglass figure. I'm sure the boys thought she was one hot mama, but she wasn't interested, especially after her encounter with Jesus.

God's promises filled Mom with passion. She soon felt compelled to make a great sacrifice, so she drew on her inner strength and packed her bags.

She said goodbye to the only home she'd ever known and set off for California. She had a goal and a determination to meet it. Bible institute and life as a missionary were calling her, and her maiden name fit her new adventure perfectly. Carmen Bravo hit the road to meet her destiny.

Carmen felt a flutter of warmth when she imagined herself in different nations, reaching the lost for Christ. She wondered, *Will I travel to China, Europe, or Latin America? Perhaps I'll go to some other far-off location and talk to people who've never heard of Jesus.*

For my mom, *where* was never as important as *who*, *what*, and *why*. She was simply committed to spreading the message of Jesus's love to anyone who would listen.

Carmen Bravo's heart to serve and inner strength equipped her well. She looked for opportunities to aid her pastors, her church, and the community where she lived. Wherever she went, her undeniable beauty captured attention, but what held their interest was her spirit.

My entire life, I've only known her to put others first.

When the opportunity arose for her to go to Bible college in La Puente, California, Carmen was excited and focused. She had no intentions of falling in love with anyone other than Jesus. No distractions. But along came a tall, dark, and handsome boy.

When Mom met Dad, Victor Torres was a Puerto Rican kid from New York, an ex-gangster who had run the streets of Brooklyn. He was also one of the only guys on campus with a car.

One day, my mother realized she'd forgotten her school books. She needed them for class, but had no way to go home and get them. She asked one of the school directors if she knew anyone who could give her a ride.

Before you could say, "God's up to something," Mom was standing with the women's director at my father's door. But the first sparks that flew between them were not sizzling with romance. She was serious and studious; he was Mr. Cool. Neither was impressed with the other. When my father saw who was at the door, he made up an excuse. "Sorry, my car is sick."

He came that close to messing up. Dad's side of the story still makes me laugh.

The director and my mom turned to walk away, but then, Victor caught a glimpse of Carmen's legs. He thought, Am I crazy? Am I gonna pass up this chance? Following respectful Bible school etiquette, he called out, "Hey, Sister Carmen. My car just got well."

And so it started. Funny how that "sick car" suddenly got well.

As they drove to pick up my mom's school books, the two young Bible students sang hymns they had learned in school. The car was filled with three-part harmony, since the director went along. Have you ever heard the expression "save room for Jesus"? Well, let's just say the director was warming up Jesus's seat.

Dad says he fell in love with my mom during that day trip. But Mom thought he had lost his mind. She most definitely wasn't on the same page.

My dad has never been one to waste time, so the next day, he decided to share his great revelation with Mom. "I'm going to marry you, and you can follow me while I travel the world sharing the gospel of Jesus Christ." He wasn't asking. He believed with that announcement, the matter was settled. Of course, my mother had a different take.

"You're crazy. I'm here for one reason and one reason only. I don't have time for boys, dating, or marriage. I'm on a mission."

But in addition to his desire to follow God's course for his life, Victor Torres was on a mission of his own. A new one. Carmen Bravo would be his wife.

Mom fought it. But Victor Torres was relentless. And as time passed, Carmen began to suspect that Victor was part of God's plan for her life. After graduation, she married him.

My mother knew nothing about the streets of Brooklyn, but she felt God was sending her, this Mexican country girl, across America to New York City. They packed, strapped all of their belongings to the top of Dad's white, two-door 1960 Chevrolet Impala, and set off on an unknown adventure.

As they drove, Carmen had more questions than answers. She didn't know what to expect, so she held on to what she was sure of: God would order their steps.

When they arrived at Teen Challenge in Brooklyn[7], they moved into a basement, where they set up house. They joined the work of David Wilkerson as his ministry reached young men and women trapped in a life of drugs and crime, like my dad once was.

I wonder how many thought, *What does this sweet little Mexican princess understand about reaching people on the streets?*

> KNOWING WHERE YOU'RE GOING IS SECONDARY TO KNOWING THE ONE WHO GOES WITH YOU.

Mom was in unfamiliar territory, and at times, the assignment left her feeling alone and scared. But she was receiving an education. She learned that knowing where you're going is secondary to knowing the One who goes with you. And it became clear that God was definitely ordering my parents' steps.

After several years of traveling and preaching together, my parents landed in Richmond, Virginia. She spoke no English and her family was thousands of miles away in her beloved country of Mexico. Her family would not be sitting around the table at Thanksgiving, or share Christmas, birthday, or anniversary celebrations with her. The familiar surroundings of youth were not part of her life anymore. She faced a new reality.

---

7. https://www.brooklyntc.org

The people Mom and Dad connected with and did outreach for became my parents' family. And my parents were all the family some of these broken men and women had ever known.

Together, Dad and Mom conquered the city as a team, Dad in the forefront, Mom in a strong supporting role. It wasn't easy for a Puerto Rican and a Mexican to minister in the capital city of Virginia. In the heart of the Confederacy, during the early seventies, they struggled. As they began to have children, there was little money for clothing, and they often wondered where their next meal would come from. How would they feed their babies? It was in those days that my parents learned to trust the God of our provision.

In the late seventies and early eighties, the United States experienced an energy crisis that forced businesses to limit their store hours so they could save on power. Because of their ministry, Mom was responsible for feeding twenty to thirty people a day. She often knocked on the doors of grocery stores. She begged the owners and managers to open so she could care for the people who'd come in off the street. Somehow, she always gathered enough.

Many Sunday afternoons, young men from our New Life For Youth program would load into a van and come to our humble little house for lunch. Often, all we had was peanut butter and beef stew. The stew did not have big chunks of meat or lots of hearty vegetables, but we were grateful for the watery canned blend.

I remember my parents praying over our meal, asking God to do a loaves and fishes miracle, so we'd have enough to go around. And we always did. But my mother never sat down until she fed everyone else first. She refused to eat until last. Always.

You might think such a level of responsibility was too much for such a tiny woman to bear, but she always had a smile on her face, like she knew a happy secret. And she did. It was the secret of faith in God, who is so much bigger than circumstances. God who was writing her story.

Mom's life included a lot of sacrifice, but as she dared to accept it, God also redeemed and rewarded her attitude of joyful giving. As a child, I took Mom's acts of service—cooking, cleaning, and encouraging—for granted. I simply didn't understand it back then.

I watched her minister to tough guys as though she was their spiritual mother. She let them know that although their birth parents may have rejected them, they were deeply loved. Strong in her faith, my mom would get down on her knees and pray to God for each one by name, as if they were her very own.

When my father traveled and preached at churches, Mom stayed at home to watch over the people in our programs, and care for us children. Her choice to do so cheerfully was evident as she sung us to sleep at night. During the day, she covered the details of the ministry. She gave up a lot to make sure others had what they needed. You could say her motto was and is, "Live to give."

> GROWING UP, WE WERE CONDITIONED BY
> THE PRACTICE OF SACRIFICE.

Growing up, we were conditioned by the practice of sacrifice. In fact, it was such common part of our lifestyle, we didn't realize we were sacrificing anything. We thought everyone lived that way.

For instance, as a little girl, I was often asked to give up my bed for people who came to us for help. Hurting people who saw us as their only hope were regular guests. But I assumed everyone lived that way, sleeping on the floor so a stranger could have a warm, soft place to sleep.

We lived in a tiny two-bedroom home. Even from a child's view, where everything appears bigger, it seemed you could walk in the front, take two steps, and fall out the back. Growing up, I also assumed everyone's groceries were delivered. I would open our front door and find groceries had magically appeared on the front porch—or so I thought.

What I didn't know then was that some of the people my parents helped often left bags of groceries on our doorstep. Out of gratitude, they wanted to make sure we had food on the table. I had no idea we were poor.

In my youth, we also experienced many miracles. As a child, I had digestive problems and required milk that needed refrigeration. It was different from the powdered variety the other children drank. It wouldn't have been an issue if we actually had a refrigerator, or the money to buy one. We had neither.

Out of desperation, my mother got down on her knees and began to pray. She didn't speak any English yet, but God knows all languages. Mom asked God for a refrigerator for my milk. Not too long afterward, a gentleman knocked on the door to deliver a fridge big enough to hold what we needed. And as an extra touch, several cases of milk came, too.

You see, God uses people to do His work. He used my parents to help others, and He also used others to help them.

The vision that became New Life For Youth began in the most unlikely of ways. God led two Latinos who came together for one common goal in the Commonwealth of Virginia. When they first arrived, there was so much division, it seemed that every church on one side was white and every church on the other side was black. Although it took years, through their work to reach the hurting, the homeless, the junkies, and the prostitutes, healing began in Richmond. It's even more miraculous when you consider we didn't exactly blend in.

Our crew wore bell bottom jeans, Afros, long hair, and tattoos. They were hippies, people of all colors, who spoke many languages. The groups we ministered to bonded through their pain, hopelessness, and addiction. We were reaching the lost—the kind I imagine Jesus wants to touch. Literally, we helped people from all walks of life, from Yale to jail.

Eventually, my father opened a church in our home. At the same time, my mother had a vision of people from every nation coming to worship together. But turning the dream into reality proved difficult.

There were many times my parents felt like giving up. They felt the sting of rejection from many in the community. Even though I was a kid, I was not too young to sense their pain.

On the most challenging days, my father expressed his frustration with talks of packing up, quitting, and letting go. Of course, those were merely the words of a frustrated man struggling to keep the ministry going.

One day, I was eavesdropping on my parents. My father told my mother, "I don't see how we can pay the staff. I'm not even sure we can keep the lights on."

Straining to hear, I pressed my ear harder against the door— hard enough that the door swung open and I fell into the next room. Like a comedy scene from a favorite movie, I was flat on my face at my father's feet.

I looked up at him and blurted, "How are we going to eat?"

Reaching down to gently lift me up from the floor, he said matter-of-factly, "God will provide."

That was good enough for me. In an instant, relief smothered my anxiety. It was as if he had handed me tickets to an all-you-can-eat buffet. If my dad said it, then I believed it. I'd seen his faith in an invisible God become sight too many times.

My parents showed me the importance of sacrifice paired with a firm belief that God will take care of your needs. Without trust, it's challenging to let go of what is in your hand to serve others.

You want to keep it for yourself and live to feed only what you want for yourself. But this is God's paradoxical truth: The more we hoard for ourselves, the less we have, yet the more we give, the more God provides, when we dare to believe.

> THE MORE WE HOARD FOR OURSELVES, THE LESS WE HAVE, YET THE MORE WE GIVE, THE MORE GOD PROVIDES.

JOCHEBED GAVE UP HER BABY SO HE WOULD LIVE

Sacrifice and faith go hand in hand, a combination Jochebed understood. I can see her now, and can almost feel her pain. How could Pharaoh be so cruel, so insecure, that he would order the death of all the Hebrew baby boys?

In the second chapter of Exodus, the Bible relates Jochebed's story of extreme sacrifice, one that ended up savings thousands of people.

The more they were persecuted and enslaved by the Egyptians, the more the Israelites' numbers grew. Pharaoh was determined to stamp out Joseph's descendants by having all male Hebrew children killed at birth. Jochebed, an Israelite, went into hiding during her pregnancy. Imagine her bittersweet mix of emotions: excitement over the upcoming birth, smothered by fear that the infant would be a boy.

As her ninth month approached, her panic surely increased. She needed a plan. A plan that would involve a baby's daring escape in a basket constructed of river reeds. The mother-to-be must have secretly gathered the papyrus reeds, dried them, and woven them into the getaway basket for her precious baby, just in case.

After he was born, she would have tried her best to quiet his sweet giggles and hungry cries. In reality, she could only do so for three months. Then she had to make the most courageous decision of her life: to trust God to take care of her sweet infant son, and pray she would not get caught. If she was discovered, the Egyptians would kill them both, leaving her other children—daughter Miriam and three-year-old son Aaron—without a mother.

Jochebed would have studied the Nile River many times, walking its banks, finding the best cast-off spot with the tallest greenery for cover. Deadly snakes, spiders, crocodiles, and other creatures must have been a concern. But she also knew her God and trusted in Him to write an impossible story.

In my mind's eye, I can see the brave mother kneeling in the reeds as she pushed the baby off into the dark Nile waters. Jochebed asked Miriam to watch the basket from afar to see what would happen to it.

Pharaoh's daughter was bathing in the Nile when she spotted the basket and sent one of her maids to fetch it. When she looked inside and found the crying baby boy, her heart filled with compassion. "This is one of the Hebrews' children," she said. Then the watchful Miriam sprang into action and offered to help the princess find someone to nurse the infant. In a plot twist that can only come from God, Pharaoh's daughter paid Jochebed to nurse the baby until he was weaned. Later in his life, God would use Moses to set the Israelite people free.

I've learned from Jochebed's example. When we faithfully let go of what we love, and release it into God's hands, He not only restores, but gives us more than we relinquished. When we dare to sacrifice, God provides a surplus. The risk is worth the reward, because God's still writing our story. In the next chapter, we will learn that Jacob knew this truth well.

I D.A.R.E. YOU TO SACRIFICE

Decide: Make the decision to surrender everything you have and everything you are to God. Sacrifice always comes with a cost, but He is the provider of surplus.

Allow: Hold loosely the people, places, things, and talents He's given you. God gave them to you, so allow Him to use them as He sees fit. Ask Him to show you what you're gripping too tightly. Let. It. Go.

Rise: Get a journal and record the ways God has come through for you in the past. If you have a prayer journal, which I recommend, make note of how God has answered your prayers. It will increase your faith, so that when God asks you to release something or someone the next time, you will remember and sacrifice again.

Enjoy: Pay attention to how God works in and through you. He often writes the most beautiful, creative and unexpected plot lines into our lives. But if we try to write over Him, we'll miss the miracles He's willing to put on our page.

Chapter 8

RISK AGAIN

I have a long-standing relationship with dieting—longer than I would like to admit. But until I learned that healthy eating must become a lifestyle, I beat myself up every time I fell into temptation. If I ate something that wasn't good for me, I scolded myself for days. Countless times, I wanted to quit due to a momentary slip. I figured, "The diet's over, and I've achieved total failure." But the truth is, I'd fallen into doomsday thinking. Know what I mean?

+ I may as well give up, my life's always going to be a mess.

+ Nothing's ever going to change for me, I'll have to deal with this forever.

+ What's the point? I can never get ahead.

+ Things always happen easier for so-and-so. Sometimes, that gal can be a real pain in my backside.

What I'm confessing is how easy it is for me to convince myself that my world is coming to an end in a matter of minutes, sometimes in seconds. The truth is, doomsday thinking rarely becomes a reality.

What I really need when I stumble is encouragement, support in the form of grace for the moment. Taking a verbal whipping, from myself or someone else, is not going to motivate me to success. I need to remember that tomorrow is another day, so I can make the decision to get up and risk living healthy. Again.

One way to set myself to action is by looking in the mirror and challenging the lady looking back at me.

+ "Unless you're willing to make a change, don't chronically complain."

+ "Wake up early and enjoy God's beauty while you're walking in the morning."

+ "Make a grocery list of healthy food, prepare it, stock the pantry, refrigerator, and freezer. Make it convenient to fuel your body well."

+ "Drink more water. No excuses."

+ "Break out of that toxic relationship so God can replace it with His best."

+ "Get moving—it's time to begin again."

No question, a few "what if's" will come to mind when you commit to risking transformational change. But fear is not going to get you what you want. "What if" is the great thief stealing our rewards.

"WHAT IF" IS THE GREAT THIEF STEALING OUR REWARDS.

One guy in the Bible risked more than a few pounds in hopes of receiving his reward. Things got a little sticky for a while.

JACOB WAITED AND WAITED FOR HIS REWARD

In Genesis chapter 29, a boy (Jacob) met a girl (Rachel). One shared glance over a well of water and BAM, love at first sip. There was only one problem.

Daddy.

When Jacob asked Rachel's father, Laban, for her hand in marriage, he agreed on the condition that Jacob work for him for seven years. And Jacob actually pulled it off. Now think about this. I don't care how much you love someone, can you imagine waiting and working for seven years of your life, with no guarantee that the other person will hold up their end of the bargain? Talk about a risk.

And if you aren't familiar with this story, you won't believe what Dad did. In the evening, after the men had a feast, Laban took his older daughter Leah to Jacob. There was no electricity in those days and it was dark. It wasn't until morning that Jacob realized he'd been duped.

Talk about a raw deal. Seven long years of service wasted, or so it would seem. But God wasn't done with this story.

Before we get into what happened next, I want to share a powerful Word from God, one that brings the risk factor down for all of us.

> The LORD says, I will give you back what you lost to the swarming locusts, the hopping locust, the stripping locusts, and the cutting locusts. It was I who sent this great destroying army against you.   (Joel 2:25 NLT)

This might sound harsh. Why would God send a bunch of locusts to destroy our crops and break our hearts? But here's what I know from watching Him work in my own circumstances and in the lives of hundreds of others. I feel like God's simply saying, "I needed to get your attention. I love you enough to take some things away so I can show you what I can give you. Sometimes I arrange a risk for faith-building, so you can experience the full scope of My reward. I will restore the years the locusts in your life have eaten— if you'll let Me finish writing the rest of your story."

NOTHING HAPPENS IN YOUR LIFE THAT GOD DOESN'T CARE ABOUT.

See what I mean by powerful? Nothing happens in your life that God doesn't care about. Jacob's concerns mattered to God as well, even when it seemed Jacob's risk had ended in collapse. But the next chapter was on the way.

Jacob was walking in God's favor. When we have an intimate relationship with someone, that happens. When we listen to them, we receive their favor.

Because Jacob talked and listened to God, and maintained his integrity by keeping his word, God covered his risk. Laban ended up agreeing to make things right, but he did require another seven years of service. And Jacob actually said yes to the risk. It paid off, too.

One of the ways people today avoid risk, and miss out on blessings, comes from avoiding service. I often challenge the women and men who come through our ministry, New Life For Youth. I tell them, "Ask the Lord, 'Please show me who I can bless today. Help me look outside myself.'"

I'm extending the same challenge to you. I know it's a risk, but if you volunteer at a local charity or your church, help a neighbor, or reach out to a stranger on the street, your life will change dramatically for the better.

I'm not saying you're going to get rich, but I am telling you a wealth of blessings will come your way. And there's no feeling like the satisfaction of making a difference in someone else's life. Just try it.

I remember a time when I asked God to use me in a special way to impact someone's life. At the grocery store, I saw a mother with three children going down the aisles. I could tell she was using all her energy to accomplish the great task of shopping while her little ones tussled and complained.

> ASK THE LORD, "PLEASE SHOW ME WHO I CAN BLESS TODAY. HELP ME LOOK OUTSIDE MYSELF."

"Don't look at me. Mom! He touched me."

I watched the woman silently pluck a box off the shelf as if it weighed twenty-five pounds.

"I don't like that cereal, Mommy. I want this one."

The lady sighed. "We can't afford that brand. You're going to have to learn to like this one."

"But I don't want that kind." The child began to scream.

When she finally got to the counter to pay, the woman's kids were louder and rowdier than before. The look on her face spoke utter discouragement, but quickly turned to horror.

As she frantically dug in pockets and pulled apart folds in her purse, I could tell she wasn't finding her money. I know what it feels like for panic to set in when you can't find something that should be where you're looking. This was my moment of answered prayer.

I cautiously entered the chaos and said to the cashier, "Please let me pay for the groceries." I could see both sets of eyes water immediately, the clerk's and the mom's. The kids were oblivious as they bickered on. But their noise didn't affect me; I was too touched by their mother's expressions of gratitude.

When I tell you there's no dollar amount that could have bought me what I felt that day, I'm not kidding. I wouldn't have traded it for Elizabeth Taylor's jewelry collection. I'm not telling you to buy groceries for every distressed mom you see in the store, but I am telling you to look for simple ways you can make a difference in someone else's life. Listen to God. He will tell you who to bless.

LOOK FOR SIMPLE WAYS YOU CAN MAKE A DIFFERENCE IN SOMEONE ELSE'S LIFE.

It's amazing how taking our eyes off of our worries by focusing on fulfilling another's needs brings us a sense of deep peace and joy. Is it a risk that someone might abuse your kindness? Sure, but their decisions are between them and God. Your job is to listen and obey. When you put your eyes on God, your own problems will begin to fade away. He restores when we step out for Him.

One area of risk for many the fear of losing someone close to them. I know from experience that when enough family and friends die around you, it feels like death is locked in on you.

When I was a girl, we buried my grandfather. Several months later, another deep loss shook my world.

Growing up in our ministry, we never had aunts, uncles, or cousins nearby. My parents left everything they knew, including their families, to reach the lost and the hurting. So the people in the programs we ran became family to me and my siblings. When people graduated through our programs, many of them chose to stay on as workers. In the late 1980s, we noticed one of our dearest staff members, Angel Cruz, started to get sick. Doctors couldn't figure out why he broke out with boils over his body, and his symptoms were like the worst flu I'd ever seen.

Angel and his wife, Lydia, were like another set of parents to us. When we were little, we would pretend to fall asleep at their house, so my parents would let us stay the night. They had children our age and many times, they were our only friends nearby.

One day, we were all excited as we left for California to attend a church conference. But almost as soon as we arrived, Angel was struck with such violent sickness that he and Lydia had to go back home. My dad sheltered us from the details of what was going on, but we knew it wasn't good.

A few months passed, and Angel's symptoms worsened. They eventually led to his hospitalization. Shortly afterward, Angel, my youth pastor and mentor, passed away and entered his heavenly home. Unbelievably, Lydia fell ill next.

Doctors diagnosed her with cancer. While his wife underwent testing, doctors gave Angel's horrific disease a name: AIDS. A past history of sharing needles to do drugs caught up with him. But he was far from the last to die. Over the months, AIDS claimed several of the people closest to us.

I was so heartbroken. To this day, I feel the loss of their passing.

Long ago, they had turned their temptations over to God, and He had delivered them from that life. The AIDS virus had wrapped its tentacles around their cells, but it did not stop them from an eternity of peace, one by one.

During this period, Pete Puig was one of my favorite people in the world. His wife, Vel, had been part of our ministry family for many years. I loved hanging out with Pete; he always made me feel important and special. Pete was in charge of the maintenance of our church building, back when we had folding chairs. As a young girl, I thought it was so cool to help Pete set up the chairs in the sanctuary and take them down later. He was meticulous about vacuuming the floors and dusting the railings.

On the day of Lydia's funeral, I stood on Pete's porch across the street from the church, watching as her casket was rolled from the hearse into the sanctuary. With his arm draped over my shoulder, Pete said something that sent chills down my spine.

In a dead calm voice, Pete said, "You know I'm going to be next."

Not long afterward, his prophesy came true. I was only sixteen. This huge accumulation of loss occurred within a small window of time. It caused a bitterness to take root in my spirit and grow. My heart became cold, so icy I couldn't cry anymore. I put an invisible wall around myself, not about to risk the feeling of losing another person I'd let in.

I poured my frustration out to God. "Why? Why would You take these great people? They gave their lives to You. You lifted them out of the streets; You broke their addiction to drugs; You restored their families. They even have children serving You now. So why did they need to go?"

Those were the questions of an innocent sixteen-year-old girl. I've since spoken to people far older who have similar questions.

I walked the dark, sad, and sometimes lonely valley of grief for a very long while. I felt alone, but after a period of time, I realized I wasn't. I believe God walked and wept beside me. When His people hurt, He hurts, too.

Today, I talk to God like I'm talking to a friend, and actually I am. He's my best friend. Sometimes, I sit in silence and look around at the trees and flowers, breathing in their fragrances and enjoying their colorful hues. When I notice the melodies of the birds, I think about the big God who created them. Their sweet songs remind me of what it says in the Bible. "If He cares about the birds in the air and the flowers of the field, how much more will He care for you." (See Matthew 6:26–32.)

> IT'S AMAZING HOW GOD WILL SPEAK TO US WHEN WE TURN DOWN THE NOISE OF LIFE AND LISTEN.

But it's in the silence when I see Him best. When He whispers to my spirit in that still, small voice. It's amazing how He will speak to us when we turn down the noise of life and listen. I've learned the importance of asking God questions, without anything plugged into my ears or any kind of electronics in my hands. Distraction is not listener friendly.

I don't know where you are in life as you read this. Are you a risk taker or a risk hater? Do you smile often and freely, or has bitterness stolen your joy? If you feel stuck on a hamster wheel of life, take the risk to jump off. If what you're doing isn't fulfilling you, dare to invest in making a difference for someone else.

God wants you to be whole and happy, living a life of exceeding abundance, not lack. Rich in relationship, wealthy in purposeful work, overflowing with joy.

Beginning again requires giving up one thing above all else: control. Dare to turn over what you fear to the only One who can restore the wasted years of your past. God sent His Son to set you free, but if you're afraid to risk accepting His offer, you are missing out on the greatest reward of all. Jesus will release you from past failures, hurts, disappointments, bitterness, and pain, if you will let Him.

No matter where you are on the journey to a new start, God is still writing your story. You may think it's too late, and you may struggle with faith to believe, but God can do a new thing in your life. We'll explore deeper depths of faith in the following pages.

As we prepare to enter the place where hope becomes reality, ask Him to heal you of any unbelief and any fear of risk. Don't let past failures define you; your greater days are before you. Your story is not over. There are more chapters to come and a great ending for Him to write. He refills His pen of promise when we dare to believe.

I D.A.R.E. YOU TO RISK

Decide: Let go of what happened yesterday. Most of what we're afraid of never happens, so don't allow fear to steal your chance for a better tomorrow.

Allow: God restores peace and wholeness, even if grief and sadness are your companions today. Accept His offer to redeem your losses.

Rise: Are you wallowing in self-pity, bitterness, or sorrow? Make sure you don't fall into the trap where these emotions become habit. Your yesterday need not be your blueprint for today.

Enjoy: If you need to develop healthier practices, don't just act on them, but do so with an intentional smile and grateful heart. Infusing ourselves with a positive mindset is a small risk for ongoing rewards.

Chapter 9

BELIEVE AGAIN

I would never trade my heritage. A lifetime of watching damaged lives transform into vibrant and respected individuals helped to shape who I am. I've seen God restore broken lives and perform miracles for thousands of people. What He promised in the Bible, He is still actively doing today.

As a young person, my faith was elevated from the powerful lessons I learned after seeing God's work first-hand. I've seen Him repair broken families and restore joy to people stripped of their dignity. Their new lives stirred excitement and emblazoned in me the expectation that God could do the impossible. Even though I wasn't immune to struggles in my own life, I believed God was able to supply all my needs. There were occasions, however, when my faith was strongly tested.

My husband and I were expecting our third child. Early on, the pregnancy wasn't much different than the two prior ones. But after my first ultrasound, I knew it was taking way too long for them to come back with the results. The tests for my first two children came back quickly. Why weren't they telling us anything?

As I finished dressing, I asked the nurse. "Did everything look okay?"

She avoided eye contact with me, pretending to wrestle a cord, and said, "The doctor will have to talk to you. She will be in shortly. I'll go get your husband, so she can speak with you together."

My mind took off, multiple scenarios playing in succession, while my heart sank and worry set in. I felt sick to my stomach as I sought out Carlos.

The doctor walked in and delivered the grim news. "Your baby's brain is not developing properly. One of the ventricles is growing too large and once they reach this size, they rarely shrink back." Then, without hesitation she added, "Rosalinda, I suggest you make the decision to terminate your pregnancy."

My husband and I looked at each other, reading thoughts as spouses do. With steely resolve in my voice, I said, "That's not an option."

The doctor pushed back. She wasn't getting me. "I really need you to understand what this is going to look like. We will have to put a VP shunt into the baby's brain and he most likely won't walk, talk, or eat normally. Rosalinda, I know you are religious, but be practical. Your life will never be the same." She then said, "I will see you in two weeks for your answer."

I left the hospital heavy with the news about our unborn child. It was the longest walk of my life. My husband held my hand until, in complete silence, we had to part ways.

He went to work. With tear-filled eyes, I drove myself to a Christian bookstore. I had been asked to sing at church in two weeks, but I needed a song, so I hoped I could clear my brain enough to find one.

While I walked the rows of books and music, I felt smothered under the weight of my emotions as thoughts of ventriculoperitoneal (VP) shunting clouded my mind. This medical procedure is used to treat hydrocephalus, which is excess fluid accumulation in the brain. Why was this happening to my baby?

There was nothing left inside me. Have you ever been there? In that place where you feel helpless, unable to change a dire situation? So drained that words won't come? A shut-down so complete that everything you do seems to happen in a slow, mechanical motion?

I couldn't even speak to God. I had no words to say.

As the painful effects of the unknown grew, we kept our heartache a secret from everyone except my parents. One of the consequences of being a PK (pastor's kid) is an acute sense of protection for the church. We didn't want our members to feel burdened or sad.

After hearing the news about our third child that day, I forced myself to listen to songs, so I could choose one for the upcoming church event. Tears poured over my cheeks as I steeled myself to begin. Heaviness squeezed me from all sides, inside and out. But once I put my ear buds in and started listening to music tracks about worshiping God, my spirit began to lift. Peace replaced my sorrow. Then I heard the perfect song.

The words of *Say the Name* by Martha Munizzi[8] soothed my aching heart. It was exactly what I needed to hear.

A few days later, when I sang it in church, I could tell people were touched. And my own faith soared with each note.

The next day, Monday, we went to see the doctor. There were a lot of unknowns as I entered the exam room. I didn't know if God would heal my baby. I didn't know if God planned to equip Carlos and me to raise a baby with special needs. I didn't know if He would decide to take our baby home to heaven, in His time. But I decided to trust Him, regardless of His choice for our family.

As we entered the doctor's office, a verse in the Bible came to my mind: *"And my God will meet all your needs according to the riches of his glory in Christ Jesus"* (Philippians 4:19). As soon as I

8. Martha Munizzi, "Say the Name," on *Say the Name* (Integrity Music, 2002).

remembered those precious words, a peace came over me. I knew that in this, my most difficult moment to date, God was more than sufficient to meet my needs.

The doctor ordered an agonizing repeat of the ultrasound. I fought tears as the cold gel swirled on my swollen belly. Even though my faith was strong, I struggled with human emotions.

Several minutes after the procedure, my doctor walked in with a fistful of papers. As I looked up at her, I noticed her face wore an expression of complete disbelief. "This is very unusual," she said. "I don't know how to explain it. But the baby is normal, the ventricle reduced in size. Everything is going to be okay."

To this day, I believe the same God who healed the leper in Luke 5:12–13 healed my baby. He is still willing and capable of moving for His people, when we dare to believe.

> GOD IS STILL WILLING AND CAPABLE OF MOVING FOR HIS PEOPLE, WHEN WE DARE TO BELIEVE.

I grew up practicing faith for others. But when I needed it for myself, I had to determine if I believed what I'd trusted for other people. It's easy to believe for someone else, but when it comes to your own dread, it's a different story.

I don't want you to think that every time I prayed, God answered my prayers exactly the way I wanted Him to. The fact is, sometimes there were periods of silence, and other times, I didn't get the answer I was looking for at all. Those times were very hard.

Women have a tendency to let so much affect us. Not only do we carry the burdens of our own lives, but since we are caring and nurturing by design, asked or not, we tend to take on the weights of others. While facing the uncertainty of my baby's future, I also wrestled with my own guilt. I wondered, *How could I be so strong for others and yet crumble in the face of my own adversity? Who could I run to, who might give me answers or comfort?*

Maybe you can relate. When we feel overwhelmed, we often search for someone or something to protect us from our feelings. We seek relief from the pressures that weaken us. But sometimes as we run for shelter, we run in the wrong direction.

+ We run under the shadow of depressions, anxieties, sin, and anger.

+ We run away from our friends and family.

+ We run away from the very freedom that we find in Christ Jesus.

Psalm 91:1–2 offers this promise: *"Whoever dwells in the shelter of the Most High will rest in the shadow of the Almighty. I will say of the* LORD, *'He is my refuge and my fortress, my God, in whom I trust.'"*

Many of us know these words, but forget to believe.

HANNAH KEPT PRAYING FOR A SON

In 1 Samuel chapter 1, we meet Hannah. Like my wrestling with faith and feelings over my baby, she dared to believe for hers. Hannah trusted God, even when it seemed her prayers were bouncing off the ceiling. Year after year, she prayed for a son. Finally, she told Him that if He gave her a son, she would dedicate him to God. It took a lot of faith on Hannah's part, but she obviously believed God was able. And He's able for you, too.

> WHEN WE PUT OUR FAITH IN GOD, OUR HOPES BECOME FUEL FOR GOD TO SHOW US WHO'S REALLY IN CONTROL.

People can intentionally or unintentionally steal our dreams. But when we put our faith in God, our hopes become more than mere words. They become fuel for God to show us who's really in control. And then it doesn't matter what people do.

Hannah could have become bitter. Not only did it seem as if her prayers were wasted, but her husband had a second wife who gave him sons and daughters, and made Hannah's life miserable. But Hannah dared to believe that God would come through. And so He ultimately did.

Even when it appeared as if He had laid His pen of promise aside, God was still writing Hannah's story. He's not finished penning your story either.

In Hannah's account, I see a pattern in her prayer that might help us all. When we feel as if our petitions are going nowhere, her model of faith can help us push through.

Hannah prayed persistently: Hannah dared to pray, year after year, despite being sorely provoked by her rival. (See 1 Samuel 1:7.)

Hannah prayed passionately: Hannah cried out to God and asked Him to remember her. (See 1 Samuel 1:10–11.)

Hannah prayed powerfully: Hannah meant and kept the vow she made to God. (See 1 Samuel 1:11, 28.)

Hannah demonstrated the kind of faith that God speaks about in three powerful New Testament passages:

The prayer of a righteous person is powerful and effective.
(James 5:16)

Devote yourselves to prayer, being watchful and thankful.
(Colossians 4:2)

This is the confidence we have in approaching God: that if we ask anything according to his will, he hears us. And if we know

that he hears us—whatever we ask—we know that we have
what we asked of him.   (1 John 5:14–15)

It's easy to look to other people in hopes that they can fix our
problems or provide our solace. But human beings don't have all
the answers. However, we know the One who does.

You may be going through something painful and hurtful
right now. You might want to give up on your marriage, your job,
or another situation. You may feel scared of the unknown. You
may wonder if your prayers are bouncing back from heaven. But
when you've reached your end, say the name that is above every
other name. *Jesus.*

You *can* trust in Him.

I D.A.R.E. YOU TO BELIEVE

Decide: Even though there are struggles in your life, believe
there is a God able to supply all your needs.

Allow: Give yourself the right to praise God in the midst of
your trouble. His Word says our thanksgiving pleases Him and
our hope will be rewarded.

Rise: One word from God can change your perspective and
help mentally move you from a valley to a mountain.

Enjoy: Let the joy of the Lord be your strength, and believe
with God, all things are possible.

Chapter 10

TRUST AGAIN

How can we trust again after people have let us down? An experience of broken promises can leave you feeling hurt and abandoned. If someone violates your confidence time and again, eventually, whether you realize it or not, the person you really lose trust in is you.

I know that sting.

You stop trusting yourself to know who you can and cannot feel safe with, so you come to trust no one. Self-preservation tactics slip in. But when you build a wall to protect yourself, that same wall imprisons you. You are locked in as much as others are locked out.

> WHEN YOU BUILD A WALL TO PROTECT YOURSELF, THAT SAME WALL IMPRISONS YOU.

This is not the abundant life God has in mind for you. He promises He will *never* fail you and He will use your past hurts to pave a way for a better future if you let Him. But trust *is* involved.

I've learned it for myself, and I've learned it from the stories of others.

One Sunday morning, I noticed the most beautiful African-American woman walk down the aisle of our church with her husband. Maybe it was her flair for fashion that caught my eye, with her white linen suit and flawlessly chosen accessories. Her hair was twisted into stylish dreadlocks, and her radiant copper skin accented a perfect posture. She appeared strong, in control, and confident.

Week after week, she and her husband attended faithfully. We saw many people, but there was something different about this couple. They immediately connected with the vision of our ministry, and their desire to serve was unmatched. Their gifts of mercy and grace were coupled with perfect timing to reach out to those who needed extra care. They visited the sick in the hospital, they comforted grieving families, and every time the doors of our church opened, it seemed, they walked through.

Before long, our two families became friends. This lovely woman's gentle kindness overflowed with compassion. You could tell she had no ulterior motives. Isn't that refreshing?

When you see someone like Josette, who appears so put together, it's hard to believe that their life was ever anything but smooth sailing. But when you get to know people, you soon discover that almost everyone has suffered something. A past hurt like betrayal, abandonment, or abuse is common—and seems to contrast a polished exterior.

> WHEN YOU GET TO KNOW PEOPLE, YOU SOON DISCOVER THAT ALMOST EVERYONE HAS SUFFERED SOMETHING.

There are some people who put on a facade to hide their pain and others like Josette who have found the courage to begin again. They risk trusting because they know that even through the deepest disappointments and disasters, God is still good.

How do you go from torment to triumph, or from trauma to trust? Josette knows.

One day over soup and salad, she and I began to share our experiences. We related to each other's heartaches and rejoiced in one another's victories. A deep, "I feel like I've known you my whole life" kind of friendship took root that day. Our tablecloth was damp from shared tears.

We laughed, we cried, we reminisced about life's challenges. Then, she shared about her deepest moment of betrayal. Having to rebuild her faith in the husband she loved. Her story surprised me.

According to Josette, the renovation work on their relationship was exhausting and sometimes trying. But she trusted God to help her overcome what sometimes felt impossible. It took time, determination, and mountains of prayer, but eventually, God taught Josette how to trust her husband once again.

She shared about her resolve to step aside and let Jesus show her how to love her man again, through the examples given in the Bible. She told me how God became the master builder in her life, as she laid aside her efforts to do it on her own. Josette said, "In spite of the injustice of the situation and my feelings of rejection, I came to understand that I had a choice. I could stay in the place of hurt, unforgiveness, and bitterness, or forgive my husband daily, making happiness my choice."

Each day, Josette learned to surrender more and more of her pain to Christ. She had nowhere to turn, but on her knees, she soon found comfort and strength. After a period of grief and growth, she learned to give her husband grace and their love grew.

I leaned across to hold her hand and we prayed. Afterward, Josette told me more.

"I didn't grasp how precious our heavenly Father is until I went through that," she said. "He never left me or abandoned me during the darkest period of my life. When I had no strength, through daily prayer, He reminded me of the unfailing love found only in Christ." She adjusted her perfectly chosen designer glasses before continuing. "When I was sick of the bondage from continuous mistrust issues, Jesus set me free."

Did Josette have reason to feel hurt and anger? Yes. Still, in spite of any justification she might have used, she began to show her husband the true love of Christ.

She said, "I knew that if God could forgive me, and Christ who knew no sin paid the penalty for my unfaithfulness, I also needed to forgive."

She understood what the psalmist meant in Psalm 46:1: "*God is our refuge and strength, an ever-present help in trouble.*"

This is good news for the rest of us. No matter what we are going through, whether we're hurt because of something we did or something someone did to us, we have choices. We are not helpless. The circumstances are not hopeless. We can choose to accept God as our strength. There are many things we do not get a choice in, but we do get to decide how we react.

> THERE ARE MANY THINGS WE DO NOT GET A CHOICE IN, BUT WE DO GET TO DECIDE HOW WE REACT.

You may not have chosen the things you endured, but you can choose to acknowledge the good that God will bring out of them. That's not my promise; that is God's lifetime guarantee.

God brought joy and laughter back into Josette's relationship. He can do the same for you, if you let Him. Put your trust in God and He won't let you down. He can even create a great purpose from your pain.

Today, Josette and her husband have an amazing marriage. They are a healed and whole couple, celebrating a friendship that runs even deeper than it did in their early years together. Through

God's guidance, there's new excitement in their relationship. Wife and husband dared to begin again as they started serving together in ministry, love, and life. There's been so much growth, that today, her husband is a natural leader and example for other men.

My dear friend sets an inspiring example. She could have sunk into the depths of her pain and built a home of misery for herself there. She could have given up, never imagining that she and her husband could feel happy. She would have missed out, if she refused to trust again.

Have you ever felt afraid to trust someone after a betrayal? Are you there now? If so, visualize God's hand stretching out to you. He understands the heartache of having someone you love commit betrayal. That's why He offers you the same option He offered Josette: undeserved forgiveness and absolute compassion. After all, whether you realize it or not, He is quite taken with you. He wants you to laugh more and cry less.

Too often, we think we have to live under the stress of our hurts, but there's another way. When you consider a past betrayal, you may think, *Why is it taking so long to get past this? When am I going to feel better?*

> THOUGH IT FEELS LIKE GOD'S TAKING TOO LONG, HE WILL ACTUALLY COME THROUGH RIGHT ON TIME.

The good news is, Jesus wants to give you victory. And though it feels like God's taking too long, He will actually come through right on time. But if you give up too soon, and choose a life of wallowing in a pit, you'll miss out on your chance to find the happiness you want. Trusting in God's goodness and mercy is not for the faint of faith because He doesn't follow our clock. Thank you, Jesus! But believing in our Father makes a lot of sense, when you understand how much He cares for us. It's not in His character to do anything outside of what is best for His children. He will not fail us. It has never crossed His mind to give up on us or the situations we're in. He has not betrayed our trust. Not once.

God taught David a lot about that.

DAVID REMAINED FAITHFUL TO SAUL

In 1 Samuel, the Bible tells us about a shepherd boy, David, who grew to become one of King Saul's most faithful men. In the eighteenth chapter, the townspeople celebrated the hero of a great battle. There was only one problem—the hero they sung about was David, not the king. Can you imagine the look on the king's face?

The stage is set for a showdown. The Israelite women joyfully danced and sang, *"Saul has slain his thousands, and David his tens of thousands"* (1 Samuel 18:7). Anger and jealousy began to burrow down into the king's heart. The tension mounted, until one day, Saul hurled his javelin at David. It missed, but Saul made his point pretty clear. David loved, honored, and served the king, but his mentor didn't reciprocate. Jealousy does some crazy things to people.

But David had a trusted protector—his best friend, Jonathan, the king's son. When Jonathan learned his father wanted to kill David, it was more than he could stand. He protected David again and again until finally, they agreed David had to go into hiding, so they said their tearful farewells.

In 1 Samuel 24, things take an interesting turn for both men. One day, Saul and his men were out hunting David, when Saul ducked into a cave to relieve himself—the same cave where David and his men were hiding out.

Even in the dark, David recognized his king. He snuck up close behind Saul and cut off the edge of his robe. After all the threats Saul made against David's life, a lot of thoughts must have run through the young warrior's head. He could easily have killed Saul as he watched the king squat in a moment of utter vulnerability.

I'm sure the idea of no longer having to live in caves and forests was pretty appealing, too.

But David made a decision of integrity. He decided not to go against God's anointed, since God was the one who had placed Saul in a position of power. Though the king acted foolishly and arrogantly, the younger man chose not to likewise act inappropriately.

David honored God and his king, trusting the Lord's promise that David would one day sit on the throne. David knew God's plan for him and he rested in the assurance that God would write his story to its rightful conclusion.

How many times do we fight impatience while we wait on God to bring to pass His plans for us? How often do we get stuck wondering if He will accomplish what we need, rather than resting in the knowledge that He will? How many times do we try to take the pen from God's hand, deciding we'd better write the story ourselves? Sometimes, we don't trust God to move fast enough.

But David trusted. He believed God made the promise and He would also make the way. David knew if he took matters into his own hands, he could forfeit God's blessing. It was God's job to take care of Saul, not David's.

> DON'T LET FEAR ROB YOU OF THE BLESSING THAT GOD WANTS TO GIVE YOU, IN HIS WAY AND HIS TIMING.

It's our job to take care of our own hearts, not to seek revenge, not to let emotions get the better of us. Don't let fear rob you of the blessing that God wants to give you, in His way and His timing. Has someone wronged you? They're God's problem, not yours. Following David's example, we have to learn how to wait on the Lord. We must trust Him not to let us down.

David's heart for God is well documented in 1 Samuel. God's provision and battle victories are listed there as well. God delivered the former shepherd boy from a lion, a bear, a giant, a jealous king, and thousands of enemy soldiers. God's faithfulness from the past fueled David's faith in the moment, all the way until God's promise was fulfilled, and David was crowned king.

If you struggle with trust issues, ask yourself a few questions:

+ What has your inability to trust gotten you? Anything good or positive?

+ What opportunities have you missed out on because you were afraid to trust again?

+ How much time and energy have jealousy and thoughts of revenge stolen?

The answers to these questions are ones Emily had to come to terms with. Unlike David, who never lost his trust in God or his friend Jonathan, Emily's trust in those she loved slipped away bit by bit.

Emily's childhood was a happy one and her family was very close. Her mom stayed at home to take care of the children while her dad took care of the maintenance at the apartment complex where they lived. Even when he was working, he was never far from home.

Emily's dad spent a lot of time with her. He taught her how to build things, quizzed her on her schoolwork at night, and helped her learn to ride a bike. Hiking up the beautiful Blue Ridge Mountains of Virginia was one of their special times together. Her father would scoop her up to ride on his shoulders high above the ground. She loved the different perspective from up there.

Every time Emily walked beside him, she gathered rocks. After marveling over each, she handed the unique and special stones up to her dad. He collected them in his pockets and carried them all the way down the mountain again. Because they mattered to her, they seemed to matter to him.

As young Christians, Emily's parents had fire and passion. Their house was always full of worship, prayer, and friends. They dreamed of becoming missionaries, but a growing family and financial responsibilities held them back. Short trips for her dad were all they could manage.

The first time her Dad went away, Emily watched the sky, wondering with each passing plane, *Is he on that one?* Finally, he came back with amazing stories of the people he had met and all the work he had done. During this period, God felt very close. Every small prayer Emily prayed seemed to bring a quick answer. Emily felt as if God was as close as her own father. Trusting God was easy then.

One day, Emily's pet bird got out and went outside. She prayed with her parents and sure enough, the next day, her beloved bird perched on a branch near her. She walked around the yard and the bird followed. It flew from bush to bush until it followed her right back inside the house. Another answered prayer.

Things changed when Emily's youngest brother was born. Postpartum depression and a thyroid disorder caused her mom to withdraw from friends and family. She sobbed uncontrollably and became someone her daughter didn't recognize.

The day her mom was hospitalized, Emily was thrust into a caregiver role for her younger brothers. To make matters worse, their dad was changing, too. The patient, rock-toting dad who used to take Emily hiking was no longer cheerful. He was distant and sullen. Emily felt like she had no one to lean on.

When her mom came home from the hospital, Emily overheard whispered conversations tainted with anger. This was a new atmosphere in their home, and Emily didn't like it. The arguments seemed to escalate weekly, until one day, her dad left.

He had fallen for another woman and walked away from his family to be with her. All of this was hidden from Emily at the time. All she knew as she entered high school was that the happy life she had known was gone. Emily no longer had a relationship with her dad. Her once peaceful mother was now full of bitterness and worry. While the family struggled to make ends meet, Emily had to grow up fast.

Since her father was out of the picture, Emily felt an adult responsibility to hold the family together. She kept going to church, but little by little, she stopped paying attention. God seemed so distant now. She felt He had stopped answering her prayers. So Emily began to doubt He was real. No more child-like faith. No more prayers. She decided God was just part of some childish imagination.

Emily was angry. She didn't understand how her parents could divorce. How could they break their promise to God, each other, and their kids? If they stopped believing in the Bible, why should she?

With a hard heart, Emily left for college, determined to live life her way and succeed on her own terms. She was going to do things differently. On campus, Emily started out focused and determined. But over time, the college goals and plans she set were replaced with friends, fun, and parties. It felt good to escape her problems. For a while.

Before long, Emily was getting into a harder and darker scene. She first experimented with party drugs. Hallucinogens and cocaine hooked her fast, and she soon wanted more. As her circle of friends changed, pills and heroin became more available. Soon, she turned her attention to heroin. She was in love, or so she thought, with that warm feeling of belonging. It drowned out everything else, including the pain from her past. But it didn't take long for heroin to begin taking its toll, and pile new pain onto the old. Emily's every waking moment was consumed with thoughts of how she would get high that day. Drugs prioritized her thoughts. She borrowed too much money. Made too many excuses. Broke too many promises. Emily was a train careening down a canyon; the crash was coming. She would do anything to avoid withdrawal sickness.

Even when Emily lost friend after friend, she still craved drugs. Several died, others disappeared into jails or hospitals, while others gave up and took their own lives.

Finally, after ten years of trying to convince herself and others she was okay, it all blew up. Emily got caught. Everything was out in the open, and the pressures increased.

Emily's mom begged her to get help, but Emily didn't want it. What she really wanted was to die. What was the point? Emily didn't think there was enough left of her to save—or that she was worth it.

But Emily eventually got tired of her mom's badgering, so she agreed to go to New Life For Youth. She screamed and dragged her feet the whole way. She couldn't imagine going to a Christian rehab when she felt like such an enemy of God. If He actually existed.

Emily's skin was a deathly gray color when she arrived at The Mercy House, New Life For Youth's women's program. But as she began to heal physically, God started to work inside of her, too, especially her heart. Every day was a new experience in trust, as Emily wrestled with the God she had given up on. Thankfully, He never gave up on her. He never gives up on any of us.

GOD NEVER GIVES UP ON ANY OF US.

As Emily sat in the Bible study classes at New Life, the Word of God started to come alive for her. While memorizing a passage of the Bible, pieces of understanding started to fall into place. She began to see her life through her heavenly Father's eyes.

For God did not appoint us to suffer wrath but to receive sal-
vation through our Lord Jesus Christ. He died for us so that,
whether we are awake or asleep, we may live together with
him. Therefore encourage one another and build each other
up, just as in fact you are doing.   (1 Thessalonians 5:9–11)

Emily had assumed that if God existed, He hated her and His
plan was for her to go to hell because of the life she had chosen.
But now, sitting on a bunk bed in her room, for the first time, she
understood His love and His sacrifice for her. After that, Emily's
life quickly changed.

She now devotes her life to helping other women find their
way out of brokenness and addiction. Through her story, others
are guided back into the arms of their loving heavenly Father.

Child-like faith? Emily's got it. Ability to trust restored? She
has that, too.

The road to trust again is not easy, although God's promises
are true and His presence is constant. But we must let Him write
our chapters, if we want the life He promised.

So you have not received a spirit that makes you fearful slaves.
Instead, you received God's Spirit when he adopted you as his
own children. Now we call him, "Abba, Father."

(Romans 8:15 NLT)

You were made for His adoration. I dare you to accept it. I
dare you to experience the same freedom Emily has now found
in Christ. Josette, too, shares the knowledge of freedom through
trust in Jesus. These women are no longer bound by past hurts.
Their memories are not yokes. They are free indeed. You can be,
too. God desires to restore your joy, your peace, your hope. What
are you waiting for? Your new life can begin today.

Every day, you can choose to put your trust in your heavenly
Father. Each day you do this, you will grow stronger and more

confident, knowing God is still writing your story. And as you'll discover in the next chapter, through His pen of promise, you need not feel alone.

I D.A.R.E. YOU TO TRUST

Decide: Determine to put your trust, your full reliance, on the God who will not and cannot fail you.

Allow: Trust God to help you tear down the "protective" walls that imprison you. Let Him be the healer, protector, and provider He wants to be for you. You are not powerless! Forgive those who've betrayed you. Trust in the God who forgives you.

Rise: Even though you may not have chosen your situation, you can grab hold of every good thing God wants to do through it. You will experience a lift when you are not bogged down by fear.

Enjoy: Find freedom from pain, jealousy, resentment, worry, and bitterness by leaning on your heavenly Father. Dare to trust in God's control, and when you do, your smile will return.

Chapter 11

CONNECT AGAIN

Ashley smiled at the young woman in the mirror, ready for her debut. With striking blonde hair and bright blue eyes that sparkled like a warm summer sky, she entered from the side stage of the New Kent County Fair pageant. Shimmering locks curled over Ashley's shoulders, her hair every inch a good southern girl's sweep. The copper dress finished off Ashley's look, dramatizing her appearance.

Her perfectly painted smile extended wide as she stepped up to the platform and waved at the crowd. Ashley floated to center stage, looking as confident as a Miss America contestant.

Ashley had already breezed through the talent competition and answered the judges' questions. It was decision time.

A deep-voiced man prepared everyone for the big announcement. "And now, ladies and gentlemen, the moment you've all waited for."

Ashley shivered, as a mix of excitement and nerves tickled her skin.

He declared the second and first runners-up, both friends of Ashley's. Then the man cleared his throat into the microphone. "And this year's New Kent County Queen is...Miss Ashley..."

Ashley heard nothing after her first name. She was the only Ashley in the running. The crowd jumped up, cheering fiercely. Ashley grinned and brushed her wet eyes while one of the judges placed the sash of honor over her shoulder. Her mind swam: I won, I actually won...

Minutes later, the hoopla swallowed Ashley up. Her parents rushed to the stage. The other girls crushed her with group hugs and congratulations. The judges came and shook her hands. Adults positioned her for newspaper photos.

"Smile," the cameraman said.

Ashley was no longer an ordinary teen—she was now a beauty queen. Proof of what her parents had always known: their baby girl was someone special.

Throughout her childhood, Ashley attended Sunday school at a local church. In every aspect, she was viewed as a good southern girl.

At sixteen, shortly after winning the pageant, Ashley went on her first mission trip. Affected by the poverty she observed, Ashley declared her plans as a beauty queen with a purpose. No doubt about it, she was going to be a world-changer. No one could stop her.

From a very young age, Ashley felt convinced that God had a special plan for her life. She knew right from wrong, and for the most part, lived out her persona as a perfect angel. But only a year after her mission trip, things changed.

During her junior year of high school, Ashley started spending time with friends who influenced a change of direction in her life. Little did she know they were leading her down a dark path. Have you ever had friends like that? Have you been a friend like this? Maybe you know exactly what I'm talking about.

At first, Ashley attended small parties that included alcohol and marijuana. Despite her beauty, she struggled with insecurities. She hid behind her smile. Desperate for acceptance and wanting to fit in with her new boyfriend, one night, Ashley gave away something she could never get back. She had always told herself she would never do it, yet in a moment of passion, she did.

A few weeks later, a test confirmed she was pregnant at age eighteen. The seed was sown. Mama and Daddy's baby was going to have a baby.

Ashley fretted over what this would do to them. As she imagined her parents' reaction to her news, a pit of nausea rolled in her gut: I'd rather die than tell them I'm going to have a baby. God, please show me a way out.

A family member told Ashley there was only one right thing to do. "You have a future to think about," this person said. To Ashley, it seemed like an answer to a prayer. Besides, adults always knew best, right?

It was a quiet drive to the abortion clinic. Ashley's mind was numb inside. She sat in silence, trying not to consider what she was getting ready to do, so she could rid her body of this "mistake."

She felt like she was moving in slow motion as she made her way up the steps of the building. Her emotions swirled in a mix of relief and nerves. She was ready to get this over with so she could move on with her life, as if none of it had ever happened.

A different Ashley walked out of the building. She had just made one more decision she could never take back. Broken and devastated by the reality of what had taken place inside, it felt as if someone had pulled her soul out of her body. How could I take the life of my baby? This is everything my parents taught me not to do, she thought to herself. I hate myself. God, I don't blame You for hating me, too.

In the days that followed, Ashley inflicted herself with condemnation, shame so strong that it became her turning point for the worse. Her regret and hurt destroyed any self-worth she might have had. Many sleepless nights, her mind raced with bleak thoughts. How could I have let myself fall into this trap?

But Ashley's guilt could not bring her baby back. So she began to search for something to separate herself further from the truth of her choice. With every attempt, Ashley convinced herself that God despised her as much as she loathed herself.

Ashley often self-medicated on street drugs, trying to run away from the reality of her abortion. But it didn't take long for her addiction to spin out of control. Three overdoses brought her to the threshold of death's door. And she felt the cut of handcuffs on her wrists during three arrests. Three was not her lucky number.

In jail, Ashley felt trapped in a pit of loneliness. Many times, she held the bars and yelled, "Get me out of here! Somebody please help me!" But if anyone heard, they ignored her pleas. Even her parents stopped going to the court hearings.

Each time Ashley returned to society, she craved a way of escape from the depression that smothered her. She turned to the staples of self-destruction: sex, alcohol, and drugs. She did anything she could, trying to fill the void in her life. Even though our lives may not resemble Ashley's, many of us have tried to fill a void with unhealthy choices.

MANY OF US HAVE TRIED TO FILL A VOID WITH UNHEALTHY CHOICES.

Several months into her spiral, Ashley became sick to her stomach. Something was wrong. She was pregnant again.

This time, Ashley decided that no matter what, she would not go down the same road twice. The price was too high and the pain too excruciating. She would not make the same mistake that cost her everything but her life—what remained of it.

But the demon of addiction was strong. Ashley did not have much in the way of support. The people who cared about her were not trained in the art of blending love and rebuke. It wasn't long before Ashley was shooting heroin into her veins again. She gave birth to a son, but within nine months, her mother took custody of the baby.

Ashley visited her son...when she had enough dope to get her through the day. She deceived and stole from her family to support her habit. That winter, her family begged her to get help.

Ashley's mom wondered, *How could our beautiful pageant winner fall so deep into this life of addiction? Where did we go wrong?* But her mom didn't disown her.

Finally, to appease her family, Ashley called New Life For Youth in Virginia. *I'll try it,* she thought. *If they see I'm keeping the lines of communication open, they'll get off my back. But I'm not plugging back into this God thing.* She continued to do drugs and steal. Then Ashley had an especially ugly drug episode.

In their own act of desperation, Ashley's family took a very courageous step to save her life.

They had her arrested.

As she sat in the jail cell, Ashley's teeth chattered so hard, it felt like they would break. She felt sick from the effects of coming down from her latest high, and knew she was close to self-destructing. If she hit the streets one more time, odds were, she'd be dead within days.

During her time in jail, Ashley thought about her ten years of addiction, and cringed at some of her memories. Then one day, she looked up and noticed something written on the wall that she hadn't seen before. In jagged scrawl, it read, "My Will Got Me Here But His Will Be Done."

Ashley had an epiphany. No matter how many times she knelt at an altar in the past, without full-fledged surrender, she would never experience freedom. So she knelt down on the cold concrete, clasped her hands together on top of the thin jail mattress, and rested her forehead against it. With tears streaming down her face, Ashley began to pray out loud. "Lord, cleanse me of my sins. Jesus, come into my heart. Forgive me for running away from You. I want a relationship with You, now and forever. I accept You as my savior and thank You for setting me free. In Jesus's name. Amen."

When she stood up, Ashley didn't look any different on the outside, but inside, she felt clean. Have you ever had a moment like this? Just like Ashley experienced, God is just a prayer away.

Upon her release, Ashley entered the women's recovery program through New Life For *Youth*. She entered The Mercy House, a women's home, and began to practice a new lifestyle of spiritual and practical applications. Today, Ashley is a completely rehabilitated wife and mother.

In 2011, I felt led by God to begin a second phase of our ministry for graduates of The Mercy House. After personally mentoring Ashley, I knew she would play an important role in this vision.

After her graduation from our women's program, Ashley became the first director of Mercy Moms, a ministry for single moms and their children. Because of Ashley's heart for service and spirit of compassion, countless women have found healing through the power of Jesus Christ. Today, she is married and serves full time in the ministry, together with her husband, Brandon, and son, Gage.

SOME PEOPLE WHO DEEM THEMSELVES UNWORTHY AND FEEL UNFORGIVABLE REFUSE TO CONNECT.

Some of the choices we make in life carry emotional guilt. We can struggle with the idea of forgiving ourselves or wonder whether God can forgive us. Some people who deem themselves unworthy and feel unforgivable refuse to connect. Isolation is a symptom of this depth of shame.

Isolation causes people to pull away from family and friends. It creates an unwillingness to look others in the eye. It rejects a caring person's attempt to help. This kind of detachment points to self-condemnation, an inner wrestling as old as time. Have you ever struggled with isolation? I know I can be tempted to isolate myself when I feel hurt.

SAMARITAN WOMAN MET JESUS AT THE WELL

History tells us of another woman who must have felt unforgivable. We don't know her name, but her interaction with Jesus has given her fame. There's much we can learn from the biblical account of the Samaritan woman at the well.

In John 4:4–42, Jesus was tired from a long walk, likely parched and covered in dust as He entered Samaria—the wrong side of the tracks in His day. His disciples have gone to buy some food and Jesus arrived at the town well around noon.

A woman approached the well to get some water, and Jesus seized an opportunity. He asked her to give Him a drink.

I imagine her brows creasing at this strange request. *"You are a Jew and I am a Samaritan woman. How can you ask me for a drink?"* (verse 9).

Like too many racial divisions we see today, the Jews hated the Samaritans. But Jesus didn't care about this woman's heritage, her skin color, her cultural slang, her living conditions, or anything else. He cared for her as a person, created in the image of God.

"Jesus answered her, 'If you knew the gift of God and who it is that asks you for a drink, you would have asked him and he would have given you living water'" (verse 10).

She must have looked confused. The well was deep and He didn't have any way to get the water. She wondered if he was greater than Jacob, who built the well.

Jesus answered, "Everyone who drinks this water will be thirsty again, but whoever drinks the water I give them will never thirst. Indeed, the water I give them will become in them a spring of water welling up to eternal life." (John 4:13–14)

That was enough for her. She wanted some of that water. Then things got personal. Jesus told her to get her husband and bring him back to the well.

You know He's a mind-reader, right?

The woman answered, "I have no husband."

Jesus agreed. *"You are right when you say you have no husband. The fact is, you have had five husbands, and the man you now have is not your husband. What you have just said is quite true"* (verses 17–18).

Now can we stop for a minute? I don't know about you, but if some guy I've never met before suddenly started to tell me my own life history, I'd have a little freak-out moment. But this Samaritan woman just rolls with it. She would have heard the stories of a coming Messiah. Her people expected a rescuer any day, so she probably had an open mind. So was she starting to suspect? Did she wonder, *Is this Him?* Her rational mind tried to make sense of the radical encounter. But the way Jesus loves doesn't always make sense.

She told Him she realized He was a prophet, so she wanted Him to clear up something for her. *"Our ancestors worshiped on this mountain, but you Jews claim that the place where we must worship is in Jerusalem"* (verse 20).

Jesus told her:

Believe me, a time is coming when you will worship the Father neither on this mountain nor in Jerusalem. You Samaritans worship what you do not know; we worship what we do know, for salvation is from the Jews. Yet a time is coming and has now come when the true worshipers will worship the Father in the Spirit and in truth, for they are the kind of worshipers the Father seeks. God is spirit, and his worshipers must worship in the Spirit and in truth.   (John 4:21–24)

I think Jesus was really trying to help her understand her need to connect with Him. Healing comes when we worship Jesus with all our strength, in our hearts, minds, and bodies. Full-fledged submission. Worship is the expression of full connection.

When the woman told Jesus that she knew the Messiah was coming and He would explain everything, He told her who He was. Just then, the disciples returned. Leaving her water jar beside the well, the woman hurried into town, telling everyone, "Come and see a man who told me everything I ever did! Could he possibly be the Messiah?" Because of her testimony, the people came streaming from the village to see Him.

> ALTHOUGH JESUS CONFRONTS OUR PAST, HE DOESN'T HOLD IT AGAINST US.

Like Ashley, the woman at the well must have carried years of guilt and shame. But although Jesus confronts our past, He doesn't hold it against us. Like He did with the Samaritan woman, He may call us out, but He doesn't condemn.

+ He doesn't discriminate based on our looks, our languages, or what side of the tracks we come from.

+ He knows every detail of everything we've ever thought, said, or done. Yet, He loves us enough that He sacrificed Himself in a slow and torturous death, so we might be forgiven and freed.

+ He has compassion for us and attends to everything we need.

+ He sees our potential beyond our pain. He makes us aware of our shortcomings, but they are not what He focuses on when He looks at us. He sees us as He created us to be.

+ He is willing to wet our insatiable thirsts and fill our voids, so we can finally feel complete. He *is* the living water.

When we are running on empty and need a refill, Jesus brings the water jar. When we believe our past sins have destroyed our future, He asks us to connect. He wants to give us a future far better than anything we imagined possible. He can do what feels impossible, by growing a purpose out of our pain.

His truth truly sets us free when we dare to connect and worship Him.

I'd like to ask you a few questions:

+ Can you remember a time when you clearly saw you were empty on the inside and had pulled away from God's refreshing presence? Is it now?

+ Have you convinced yourself that you've done something unforgivable, but not asked God directly if He feels the same?

+ How do you refill with God's Holy Spirit each day? Are you allowing Him to quench your daily thirst?

Maybe you feel like you are in a spiritual desert. If so, I've got good news: Jesus wants to fill you up.

You may never get over the choices you can't take back, but you can get through them. The process of forgiveness begins with surrendering your heart to Christ. Allow Him access to your deepest wounds, and dare to believe God's promises that through His Son, you are forgiven.

Dare to connect by spending time in Jesus's presence, reminding yourself that He died on the cross for you. He loves you that much. Dare to connect by praising Him for doing for you what you couldn't do for yourself.

Because of His sacrifice, once and for all, you are made whole. You no longer have to suffer the price of your sins. God does not want you stuck in spiritual paralysis, trapped by guilt. Does any of this ring with hope for you?

> GOD DOES NOT WANT YOU STUCK IN SPIRITUAL PARALYSIS, TRAPPED BY GUILT.

Maybe you didn't have an abortion, but you carry the burdens of other decisions. Whatever your past, do not waste one more second letting it ruin your present. It can only destroy your future if you allow it. Like He did for Ashley, God wants to re-write your story, too.

For all of us, the freedom we search for is available through Christ. Anywhere, anytime, anyone can confess, accept, and believe that connecting with Him will make all things new. Worshipping Him daily releases the ink in His pen of promise.

Ashley learned that her healing required a daily surrender. Jesus paid her price on Calvary, but the daily choice to accept this precious gift was hers.

> *There is therefore now no condemnation to them which are in Christ Jesus, who walk not after the flesh, but after the Spirit.*
> (Romans 8:1 KJV)

Take a moment and inventory your heart. If you think you have gone too far, you may not have a full understanding of the promises of God. He is ready to bestow His gift of grace on us. Healing begins with accepting the Father's forgiveness. Allow yourself to connect with Him again.

Tell the Lord why you feel so distant from Him, where you took the wrong road, and lay it down at the feet of Christ. Take responsibility—He never left you, you left Him. You may not be a former addict like Ashley. You may not have let lust rule your past. But at some point, we all pulled away from the grace that heals.

No matter what your story, I can assure you, God's willing to write more. And your new chapters will be better than the former.

YOU WEREN'T CREATED TO DO LIFE ALONE.

You weren't created to do life alone. Connect with your Father, His Son Jesus, and His Holy Spirit. Connect with people who can and will support you with a blend of love and accountability. Complete healing is possible. You have free will to decide whether to accept or reject God's offer of healing. It's up to you. If you feel dead inside, will you dare to get up and walk once again? Stay tuned, and discover how.

I D.A.R.E. YOU TO CONNECT

Decide: Stop pushing away caring and godly people who speak truth. To begin again, you need to surround yourself with those who will not tell you what your itching ears want to hear.

Allow: Let God forgive you. There are only two things He cannot do: lie and break His word. But He gave us free will to choose for ourselves. Though His forgiveness is readily available, He cannot and will not shove it down our throats.

Rise: Move beyond your past and consider how God might bring about a purpose beyond yourself from it. He's willing to make crowns of beauty out of the ashes of our lives.

Enjoy: Newfound freedom is yours, when you dare to connect with Christ. Get up with a song in your spirit and joy in your heart. He waits for you to wake up each morning, just so He can spend time connecting with you.

Chapter 12

HEAL AGAIN

Sometimes, miracles are disguised by odd behaviors.

In John 11:1–44, we meet two sisters, Mary and Martha, whose brother, Lazarus, has become deathly ill. Of course, the sisters desperately wanted their brother to be healed, so they sent an urgent message to Jesus. Having developed a personal relationship with Him, they knew Jesus could make Lazarus well.

But Jesus stayed where he was for two days. When He finally went to see His friends, Lazarus had been in the tomb for four days. Both sisters told Him that their brother would still be alive if He had been there. Mary and her friends weep so much that Jesus breaks down and weeps, too.

Have you ever felt this way? Wondering where Jesus was when you called Him? Have you ever thought, *Has He abandoned me?*

During times of grief and extreme worry, when I'm stripped bare of any masks, I've wondered, *Where were you when I called, Jesus?*

JESUS HURTS WHEN WE HURT

I think we've all fallen into the trap of feeling like God should respond within our timeframe. It's easy for us to believe that if

He doesn't respond right away, He's not listening. But we must be careful not to judge God's seemingly delayed response with our preconceived ideas. We can't know how He should answer us. But in this biblical account of Lazarus, we learn something about Jesus's natural reaction to our pain. When we hurt, He hurts, just like He did over the loss of His friend.

GOD'S TIMING IS ALWAYS PERFECT.

It may not be in our time and we may not always understand the delays, but God's timing is always perfect. Mary and Martha expressed their desire for Lazarus's healing, but Christ had so much more in mind. He had a miracle in store for them, and raised Lazarus from the dead. He may have a miracle waiting for you, too.

We may not comprehend God's delays while He's writing our stories. We are sometimes puzzled by what we're going through. But just like Jesus wept when He saw others mourning for Lazarus, He has wept for your pain, your hurts, and your sorrows. He cares deeply for you.

Victoria learned that up close and personal.

She was one of five kids. From the outside, her life may have seemed typical. Just another American family living in Virginia.

She grew up on Organ Hill in the heart of Richmond. Their house was wedged between Hollywood Cemetery—where Presidents James Monroe and John Tyler, as well Confederate President Jefferson Davis, are buried—and streets where Civil War battles once raged.

Victoria's father was a blue-collar factory worker and her mother was a stay-at-home mom. They did the best they could to keep their kids in school and out of trouble. Every weekend, they would get dressed up and go to a local church. Sundays followed a predictable routine: church in the morning, poker in the evening.

Victoria recalls, "The memory is imprinted on my mind. The leaves had started turning vibrant colors of scarlet, orange, and rust. Their beauty was something I felt as well as saw. It was a Sunday afternoon, not too cold outside, not too hot, just perfectly right. I felt at peace in my lavender bedroom. I lined my pretty dolls across my bed, each with its own special name.

"My folks were busy playing penny ante poker, following their Sunday afternoon ritual. I had been running around the house but I needed to go to the bathroom. So I ran upstairs and cut through the bedroom to the bathroom like I always did. I didn't know that in a few more steps, my life would change forever.

"My older brother was hiding in the room. At first, I didn't realize what he was doing, although I felt scared when he trapped me and began to fondle my body. I panicked. I knew this was wrong, but he was also older, bigger, and much stronger. He threatened me and told me Mom and Dad would send me away if I ever told. He said I would never see my family again. I didn't know what to do.

"Terrified and shaking, I ran away, heart racing. I couldn't catch a full breath. In actuality, I struggled to breathe for years after."

That day wounded and scarred Victoria's life. For six more years, she struggled with panic attacks and daymares. She tried her best to live normally, but life kept punching her in the gut.

Later, Victoria's mother was in a car accident, and her father decided to move the family from the city to the country. Victoria only knew one way to survive. She stuffed her emotions and memories. She blocked out the dreadful pain that haunted her. She lived on the outside of herself, as if the pain didn't exist, but the daymares became more and more overwhelming.

Finally, in Victoria's senior year of high school, she opened up to her teacher. She couldn't take it anymore and needed someone she could trust. But the day Victoria's parents were informed, everything changed when she got off the bus.

Victoria's parents kicked her brother out of the home, but her mother blamed Victoria for the abuse. The wounded girl in her longed to be comforted. Everything inside her was broken. Her throat swelled and her eyes burned from the tears. But even her mother was against her, so who could console Victoria through this ordeal?

Victoria turned to self-medication. She needed to escape.

Victoria had a choice to make. She had every reason to let her circumstances hold her back. After all, her pain was real and her emotional scars came from genuine injuries. She had a right to feel hurt, upset, and distraught. The perfect tools for building emotional shackles—and she wore them for a while. But Victoria wanted to break loose.

After years of struggling with depression and addiction, Victoria tired of the emotional shackles that sliced into her soul. Sometimes, the darkness felt so suffocating, she woke up in the middle of the night struggling to breathe.

In her most broken hour, Victoria knelt down and allowed her tears to spill onto the floor. She begged God to heal her and invited Jesus to enter her heart. Immediately, Victoria felt something was different.

Victoria said of that moment, "It was like coming to the surface of the water after a deep dive and finally breathing again. After almost thirty-seven years of feeling dead inside, I now felt alive."

In Christ, Victoria finally found the deep healing she sought. That same hope is available to all of us.

Victoria came to recognize that the process came with its own challenges. She understood that surrendering had immediate benefits, although it wasn't an immediate fix. But Victoria still dared to accept Christ's offer of healing. She put away the negative emotions she could have clung to, so God could write a better story over her life.

Let all bitterness and wrath and anger and clamor and slander be put away from you, along with all malice. Be kind to one another, tender-hearted, forgiving each other, just as God in Christ also has forgiven you. (Ephesians 4:31–32 NASB)

Victoria dared to believe that her sins had been forgiven and that the promises in the Bible were true. Even for her. Her shackles fell away when she dared to begin again.

Shortly afterward, Victoria drove through her old neighborhood on her way to her new house. It only added a few minutes to take the route, and she enjoyed the beautiful drive. But soon, Victoria's brain slipped into the painful memory of what her brother had done.

As she was driving, a question popped into her mind: *What are you doing?*

Victoria felt instant conviction, and immediately did two things to reset her mind. First, she took a practical approach, and turned the car in another direction. Removing herself from the trigger. Second, Victoria focused on the spiritual truths of God's work in her life. Victoria knew she had experienced healing from her past. She understood that Christ's sacrifice had set her free. Instead of allowing her mind to wander, she began to thank Him for forgiveness, freedom, and liberty. She reviewed the origin of her healing.

Victoria had encountered her initial healing at her original point of surrender. Then, Christ had given her the freedom she was searching for. But Victoria also needed surrendering resets, times when she intentionally stopped focusing on her past and began to look forward to her new life in Christ. Victoria came to understand that her memories could be viewed like scenery from her car. She could look through the windshield and see the panoramic view of her life unfolding ahead. Or she could glance through the small rearview mirror of her past, and allow it to hinder her forward motion.

Do you allow painful emotions to replay in your mind? Maybe you don't think playing that old song repeatedly causes any harm. Do you realize how often you retell the story of your hurt? Each time you do, you are taking yourself back to the place God delivered you from. He's done with that story. He's looking ahead to your new one. Are you?

Too often, we ask ourselves why we still hurt and why we can't put a past behind us. We even say to ourselves, I hate the event that brought me so much pain.

It's healthy to "get it out" and share our deepest hurts. But we risk getting stuck in the past if we move beyond healthy venting and into a toxic reliving. There is a fine line between rehearsing our pain and sharing the pain to release it for healing.

DON'T TAKE YOURSELF DOWN AN UNNECESSARY "MEMORY LANE."

Don't take yourself down an unnecessary "memory lane."

Do you drive by the house of an ex-spouse or regularly visit a restaurant that held memories of your past?

Are you crying in your drink as you replay your despair?

Are you listening to "your" song?

Are you re-reading the letters of your past?

Do you find yourself wasting hours, flipping through your social media?

In Matthew 8:7, we find a promise: *"Jesus said to him, 'I will come and heal him'"* (NASB).

> ## REAL HOPE FOR REAL HEALING IS SOMETHING ONLY GOD CAN OFFER.

It's up to us to allow God to heal us. No matter how big our storm, God holds out His loving arms to cradle us in His safe embrace. Real hope for real healing is something only He can offer. We simply must say yes. Are you ready to say yes? Don't delay your healing another day.

God is the grand restorer. He goes beyond our expectations and takes care of us in so many ways. He honored Victoria's attitude of humble submission. He healed her from her brokenness. He wants to do the same for you.

Today, Victoria says one of the secrets for her continued strength is her private time with God by reading the Bible. She now knows that no matter what comes her way, He will not abandon her, He will not forsake her. "In fact," she says, "I am counted among His children. I have value. I have worth. And I have a purpose." Victoria's words are worth repeating to yourself.

> *The LORD will guide you always; he will satisfy your needs in a sun-scorched land and will strengthen your frame. You will be like a well-watered garden, like a spring whose waters never fail.* (Isaiah 58:11)

Take a moment and talk to God right now. If you feel shackled by your pain, get a piece of paper and a pen or pencil, and write about those things that weigh you down. Make a choice to release them to God. Tell Him you are ready to be set free. Ask God to forgive you for not trusting Him before now. Ask Him to remove any heavy weights from your life.

Too many people don't really understand the term "surrender." It means to "cease resistance and submit to authority," or "to give up completely or agree to forgo especially in favor of another." When you surrender, you give up and give it all to Jesus—you lay all your pain and hurt at His feet, as He invites us to. He wants it all.

> WHEN YOU SURRENDER, YOU LAY ALL YOUR PAIN AND HURT AT JESUS'S FEET, AS HE INVITES US TO.

In fact, Jesus tells us:

Come to me, all you who are weary and burdened, and I will give you rest. Take my yoke upon you and learn from me, for I am gentle and humble in heart, and you will find rest for your souls. (Matthew 11:28–29)

Jesus will cradle you and heal your heartaches. He will wrap His arms of love around your heart. He can see everything you're holding on to, so don't be afraid. He's got this!

Once you've gotten alone with God and written your list on that sheet of paper, take one more step. Read that list out loud to Him as a praise. Thank God for your freedom as you list each specific area you are trusting Him to release you from. Then throw that sheet of paper away. Release the past into the hands of Jesus and don't pick it up again.

God desires all to be well in our lives and for us to live free through Him. So I dare you to heal again. It's not time to give up, it's not time to rest—it's time to be restored and move forward. It's time to begin again!

When I was going through a personal challenge in my life, I remember a few simple words that someone dear and close to me said. "You can make it. You will find healing. And you will get through this."

GOD DESIRES ALL TO BE WELL IN OUR LIVES AND FOR US TO LIVE FREE THROUGH HIM.

It was God's desire and promise for my life, but I had to take action. Healing required me to choose to walk in that victory every day. It would have been easy to let past failures discourage me, but I made a bold decision to overcome. I no longer wanted to remain in my place of disappointment. I was ready to heal again.

I don't know your hurt, your sorrows, or your regrets. But I do know a God who loves you so much that He sent His son to die on the cross so that you could be free. Free from your hurt and free from your past. Just because you had a failure in life doesn't mean you cannot try again. Failing doesn't make you a failure.

As a young teenager, I went on a hiking trip with a friend. She took me to a ropes course, and I thought it was the coolest thing I'd ever seen. We hiked the mountain, ate natural foods (I thought, *Great, I'm eating squirrel food*), and I learned many amazing lessons that day. One of them was how to trust others. We did an exercise where the group stood in two lines facing each other, but one person had to climb up a wall. I gulped when they chose me.

The leader instructed me to face the wall, close my eyes, and fall back into the arms of the people. I was known as somewhat of daredevil, but this day proved different. For the life of me, I couldn't bring myself to fall back into the arms of the people. In my mind, I knew I had been hurt and let down by others, which scared me to the point that I had a hard time trusting. But I wanted to heal from that. I didn't want to feel afraid anymore.

So I breathed deeply to calm my nerves, folded my arms across my chest, took another deep breath, and fell back into the unknown. It was a huge relief when I felt their arms catch me. It was like lying on a warm, solid blanket.

That simple little exercise erased doubt in my heart and mind. I realized that many people do care and they're not out to hurt me. The actions of some do not define the hearts of all. I developed instant trust when the other participants didn't let me fall to the ground.

Now I'm not saying you should go gather your friends and ask them to get into line so you can fall back into their arms. However, I am going to tell you that God has His arms outstretched. Dare to let go and heal. When you do, God will begin to build your story. He's not done writing yet.

I D.A.R.E. YOU TO HEAL

Decide: Understand that surrendering your past has immediate benefits and that your sins are forgiven. Decide to accept that the promises in the Bible are true for you.

Allow: Let the love of God embrace you. He will fill you to overflowing, so you can enter into the liberty only available from His perfect healing.

Rise: Don't let your past hurts, disappointments, and rejections hold you down. God truly loves you and wants to take you to a place beyond injury. He will lift you up if you are willing to fall back into His arms.

Enjoy: Rest in the embrace of a Father who adores you. No matter what anyone has done, you are free to know unconditional love.

Chapter 13

BUILD AGAIN

My husband, Carlos, and I were both born with an entrepreneurial spirit. We know what it feels like to work hard and bring home the bacon. But we have also faced conditions so desperate we were forced to live through unemployment. Financially for us, these were the worst of times.

Walking into a lending institution and sitting in front of a loan officer is daunting under the best conditions. But when you're desperate to refinance your home so you can lower your monthly payments, it can be both humbling and humiliating. After dealing with back-to-back health crises with our son, however, we had no choice. Carlos and I swallowed our pride and made the appointment.

The day we met with the owner of the mortgage company, the look on my husband's face said his mind was spinning as much as mine. The employees impressed us with their kind demeanors. All of their people had amazing sales abilities. Everyone on their team showed genuine interest in our needs and it struck a chord in my heart. Two questions popped into my mind:

I wonder if they're hiring? Wouldn't this be a great opportunity for Carlos to start the new career he's been searching for?

The possibility that this might open up an employment opportunity for my husband gave me hope. We sure could use the money.

Soon after, God opened the door and Carlos got a job at the mortgage company. Within six months, he was the top salesperson at the agency. He'd found his niche.

As Carlos flourished, we began to pray that we would have our own company one day. But we got a surprise. Carlos was offered a partnership in another company, which included half the company's profits. We jumped at the opportunity.

For over a year, he worked with his partner to build a new office from the ground up. This was a place of training for my husband. We still believed God would answer our prayers and let us run our own mortgage company one day.

In our family and ministries, integrity holds a high place of importance. So when the day came for Carlos to quit his old job, he did so with the highest degree of integrity. He refused to draw any of the employees from the company he was leaving, so we had to start from scratch.

We rented a little office space near our home and launched the Home Mortgage Depot. We didn't have a lot of money for advertising, but we had an idea to involve our son and daughter in the commercials. The sweet voices of our kids and their funny little lisps connected with consumers. The commercials generated a tremendous amount of business for our family company. People all over town knew our kids from those ads.

Soon, we outgrew that little space and decided to build our own brick and mortar office building. Carlos worked day and night. He spoke with customers, hired new employees, and conducted a company devotional every morning. I often chuckled when I walked into his office, telling him, "Honey, you do more ministry than business here."

It was hard for him to argue, considering the number of couples he prayed with and the hearts he helped turn to the Lord. I caught myself admiring him. I'd watched Dad do the same thing all my life. I knew the long-term impact someone with a passion and drive for ministry could make. I told Carlos, "You know you're a pastor and we have a calling on our lives."

He wasn't quite convinced enough to agree with me. Yet.

Carlos made a commitment early in his life to put his finances in God's hands. He was a giver, a tither, and most importantly, he had a desire to help people put their houses in financial order.

Our business grew and soon, he had over twenty employees working for him. Our gross revenues catapulted to millions of dollars in sales. The extra income afforded us many material things. We built a home for us, and were able to buy several rental houses. I appreciated how giving my husband was. He blessed others and poured into the various branches of New Life ministries.

But as often happens, the more the business grew, the less time we had as a family. Financially, we could vacation anywhere, but it was almost impossible to carve out time. I guess you could say we were money-rich and time-poor.

As the business demanded more and more of our time, we would talk about leaving it all behind and going into full-time ministry. God had placed that call on our lives when we were first married.

> WE MIGHT IGNORE HIM, BUT GOD'S PURPOSE FOR US DOESN'T CHANGE.

We might ignore Him, but God's purpose for us doesn't change. Eventually, He pushes harder. It was starting to feel like it was time to make that move.

One day, Carlos went to the doctor for a routine visit. I sat in the waiting room and watched the news during his exam. When he came out, he knew something was wrong with me.

I was glued to the TV screen with an expression of shock and horror. I knew enough about the mortgage industry to know we were in trouble. Our world was about to shake with volcanic force. Without taking my eyes off the program, I said to Carlos, "Baby, you'd better sit down." I failed to ask him how his doctor's appointment went.

CNN's breaking news reports told of collapsing banks. They predicted the fall of the mortgage industry. I clutched Carlos's arm and said, "How is this going to affect us?"

I can't remember exactly what he said. But I know what happened next. The financial fall of 2008 hit so fast and hard that it caused panic and financial turmoil around the world. And it devastated us personally.

At the start of the recession, we had over $1.5 million in buildings. You can imagine what the monthly expenses were like. But like a tornado sweeping through without a warning siren, we had no time to prepare. Within one week, loans stopped closing. Insurance companies and the federal government would not back mortgage loans. And although we didn't know it yet, life was going to take another turn.

The pressure my husband carried during that time was unbelievable. Men and women worldwide crumbled under the stress. Some took their own lives. A friend of mine lost her husband, and yet another had a heart attack.

Eventually, we made the decision to leave our home, forced by the financial squeeze. The home sold for exactly what we paid for it, but we couldn't recoup the $150,000 we'd put into it. We were still grateful that we didn't lose the home altogether. Still, the storm was not over.

Our nights were riddled with anxiety. There were times I couldn't sleep, and after tossing and turning, I would snuggle into Carlos's arms and ask him to pray for me. His focused faith in those moments gave me the strength to rest. There were other times, though, when my husband could not rest. It was then that I leaned over and prayed that God would give him peace.

It all felt so unfair. Why was this strong Christian man who had dedicated himself to obeying God facing such a devastating situation? Why was he stripped of control from a situation he did not cause? Total loss causes a helpless feeling—until you fix your attention on the source of true help.

One day, as we held hands and talked, Carlos and I agreed to stop looking at the situation and focus on our Source. We decided to trust in the Lord and believe that God would help us begin again.

That meant putting everything my husband had worked to build at the foot of the cross. This great husband, father, and businessman who had made it a habit to honor God and act with integrity committed to laying it all down.

We couldn't help asking ourselves, Why was this happening to us? I think the situation would have been easier to deal with if we thought we were getting what we deserved. But the recession was completely out of our hands and we were helpless to fix it. We were caught in the line of fire, completely reliant on God to bring the water hose.

> WHEN OUR PLANS CRUMBLE,
> WE HAVE NO CHOICE BUT TO BEGIN AGAIN.

Of course, all of us are completely reliant on God to come through in all things, but in troubles as dramatic as the recession, we count on it. When our plans crumble, we have no choice but to begin again. Whether we've lost a job, a relationship, have had health issues, or faced any other major crisis, the timeline does not catch God off guard. Everything's going according to plan. The building period and the demolition process are all part of preparing us for our purpose. This rough terrain is where we pick up the tools necessary to move on to the next level. But first, there's a test of faith. And believe me, it was a TEST!

Before the financial market imploded in 2008, we had a savings account with $100,000 in it. We hoped to use it to keep the company afloat by paying mortgages and employees. But very quickly, the balance dwindled to $2,000. From that point, we vowed we would not go into our next season with debt from our last.

> IF WHAT YOU HAVE IN YOUR HAND IS NOT YOUR HARVEST, IT MUST BE YOUR SEED.

We were visiting a church one Sunday and during the service, the pastor took up a special offering for their building project. I knew what my husband was thinking: If what you have in your hand is not your harvest, it must be your seed. I smiled. I didn't even have to ask. I didn't know how, but I knew we were going for broke.

When Carlos and I talked about it later, we decided to give $1,000 from the last of our savings to my sister's ministry in Africa. The other $1,000 would help to build a gym for the children in the church. Our final balance? Zero dollars and zero cents. We were planting seed for a big miracle.

When we got back to Richmond, we still hadn't unpacked our bags when the phone rang. It was odd to hear a stranger's voice on the other end because I never give out my home phone number. The man asked, "Are you Mrs. Rivera?"

Feeling a little hesitant, I said, "Yes."

"Is your husband still selling his mortgage building?"

"Yes," I told him.

"I represent a doctor who wants to buy your building. How quick can you move out?"

When I hung up, my feet left the floor, and I yelled up to Carlos, "They're going to buy the building and give us full price."

Several weeks later, my husband got a phone call. From the other room, I could hear Carlos saying, "You're kidding. You're kidding. Come on, you're kiddin'!"

I couldn't wait to hear what the caller was telling him. When he hung up, he was grinning like a kid with a secret. He explained that our county's access to their water was behind the tiny 600-square-foot rental house we owned and hadn't been able to sell. The county wanted to buy the house to knock it down. And they were willing to pay full price.

That day in the church we visited, we caught a vision of how we could begin again. As a result, we had given all we had in savings, $2,000. We sowed two seeds, and up sprouted two different miracles.

The process of beginning again was like nothing we'd ever experienced. We cried a lot and there were many moments of silence over dinner. To say it was humbling is an understatement. But ultimately, our faith was met by God's faithfulness.

It didn't take long to realize that our house was too big and more than we could really afford. So we sold it and moved to the city of Richmond about a month before Christmas. For the first time in our married lives, we were renters. We were welcomed to the neighborhood by burglars who broke into our home and stole our jewelry, including my husband's wedding ring, and the children's laptops and video game stations.

> YOU'VE MADE THE ENEMY NERVOUS WHEN
> THINGS GET RIDICULOUSLY BAD,
> WHEN ONE THING AFTER ANOTHER FALLS APART.

One thing we had learned through our years together was to recognize the signs when you've made the enemy nervous. When things get ridiculously bad, when one thing after another falls apart, he must be one mad dude.

We ended up moving into a basement as big as my walk-in closet in our previous home. We gave our children the upstairs section of the house. I could see how our housing situation pained Carlos, and it deepened my sadness. Men were created to guide, guard, and govern, so when a man is struggling to provide for his family, he can feel overwhelmed.

The next spring, we were able to buy a fixer-upper—and that's being gracious. Nothing in the kitchen worked and every ceiling in the house was on the floor. There was even a family of raccoons living under the roof. But watching one of our favorite television shows on HGTV inspired us to get to work. We figured if they could do it, we could, too.

Our renovation project breathed new life into my husband. Friends and family members now knew what we had gone through. And many of Carlos's friends who owned construction companies dropped off windows, new bathroom fixtures, countertops, and glass doors. We had purchased the house for $130,000, and thirty-six months later, we sold it seven days after putting it on the market—for $260,000. Once again, we were humbled when our faith was met by God's favor. He wasn't done giving to us yet. He was still writing our story. And He's still writing yours.

Back when we owned the mortgage company, Carlos and I hoped to one day live in a hacienda. These Spanish-style homes are hard to find in Virginia, but we dared to dream. As we were preparing our fixer-upper for sale, we scanned an online Realtor's site. We were shocked to see our dream hacienda with two acres for sale.

We jumped in the car and put a contract on it the first day for $150,000 below assessment. They accepted our offer. We wondered if God remembered the money we thought we lost on our old home, and decided he would restore it to us in this new place. The $150,000 below assessment was an exact match for what we had lost on our previous home.

Our hacienda came with some history. All the ironworks were imported from Mexico, and the doors and lighting were built by the president of PBS. But our dream home didn't come without its issues. It was another fixer-upper. Through the years, the house had lost its luster. But frankly, after evicting a raccoon family of five from the last place we lived, I wasn't intimidated by the work that needed to be done.

Today, after God wrote that part of our story, we still live in our dream house.

Through all of this, Carlos never lost his faith in God. In fact, the tumultuous seasons made him stronger. We began to appreciate things as a family in an entirely new way. And Carlos felt a tug into full-time ministry. He began a program at the church called Frontline, which started off with a small group, but grew fast.

Today, these men meet every week, studying the Word of God. They mentor each other and take their growing faith back into their homes. God is using my husband to start a revolution in the hearts of men.

When we look back, we are amazed at how money and things trapped us. We were tied to work and rarely had time to enjoy what our possessions provided. Now we live on much less, but we have the opportunity to travel the world, sharing the gospel of Jesus

Christ. To date, we've visited over twenty-one countries, including Turkey, Russia, Brazil, Africa, Wales, Ireland, and Scotland.

I realize now that we wouldn't have moved, because of fear or feeling unsure, until we had to. We had always felt a call into full-time ministry, but until the demise of the mortgage company, we wouldn't budge. Sometimes, to get us from one place to the next, the Lord allows a situation to push us in that direction. God will even use a wrecking ball to demolish your good life, if that's what it takes to force you into building your godly life.

> GOD WILL EVEN USE A WRECKING BALL TO DEMOLISH YOUR GOOD LIFE, IF THAT'S WHAT IT TAKES TO FORCE YOU INTO BUILDING YOUR GODLY LIFE.

GOD'S PLAN DIDN'T MAKE SENSE BUT GIDEON OBEYED

A man named Gideon understood God's wrecking ball. It cleared the way for a God-sized miracle. In Judges 6, the Bible tells us a man named Gideon was threshing wheat in a hidden place. Then he looked up and saw an angel sitting under a tree. The angel told Gideon that he was a brave man, the Lord was with him, and he was going to save his people from the Midianites.

How could that be? Gideon's family was poor and he was a nobody. But the angel assured him that the Lord would be with him.

After more dramatic interactions with God—you will want to read the full, fascinating account for yourself in the book of Judges—Gideon gathers an army and thinks he's ready to save his people. But God turns things upside down.

The LORD said to Gideon, You have too many men. I cannot deliver Midian into their hands, or Israel would boast against me, "My own strength has saved me." Now announce to the army, "Anyone who trembles with fear may turn back and leave Mount Gilead." So twenty-two thousand men left, while ten thousand remained. (Judges 7:2–3)

Stop and think about the reality of that. Can you imagine what poor Gideon thought as two-thirds of his fighters abandoned him? The lines of able-bodied men slinking away must have stretched for miles. Gideon might have thought, *Lord, I thought you said you were with me!*

So Gideon restructured the plan with only ten thousand warriors. And in Judges 7:4–7, the Lord turns things upside down again. He tells Gideon he still has too many men, so He will select the ones he wants for the battle by the way they take a drink of water. The Lord wants those who cup the water in their hands and lap it up, not those who kneel down and stick their mouths into the water to drink.

Just being honest, if I were Gideon, somewhere in my mind, I would have questioned God's plan or my sanity. But Gideon did exactly what God instructed.

Only three hundred men slurped water from their hands. The majority got down on their knees to take a drink. Through this sorting process, God culled the vast army Gideon had gathered— but why? What was wrong with Gideon's idea? After all, it made more sense...didn't it? Isn't it humorous when we think we know more than God?

It may be that God chose quality over quantity.

Gideon sent nearly ten thousand men away and marched on with his little band of three hundred brave, focused guys. God did not need a large army, only a few careful, bold men who would do exactly as their leader commanded them. Carrying trumpets and jars with torches hidden inside, they surrounded the enemy camp at night. Then they made quite a racket, breaking the jars, blowing the trumpets, and waving the torches, crying out, "The sword of the Lord and of Gideon!" That set off panic in the camp—and the enemy soldiers ended up slaughtering each other.

By winning the battle with a lot fewer men, God was glorified and the people came to know He was the one true God.

We discussed trust and belief before we explored building again. That was quite intentional. You cannot face the unknowns of where you're going without first learning to trust the One who goes before you. The building blocks for God's most exciting stories are made of faith.

Your own story is being revealed right now. He is going ahead of you and preparing the way. But remember, construction often looks like destruction when you start. Sometimes, God removes the very things we think we need in the same way He dwindled Gideon's army—to show us His power.

> SOMETIMES, GOD REMOVES THE VERY THINGS WE THINK WE NEED TO SHOW US HIS POWER.

Gideon had to sacrifice what he thought he needed to win, but Gideon's obedience and willingness to do God's thing God's way is something many people still talk about today. His story is still making an impact more than three thousand years later because of what he allowed God to build from nearly nothing.

We think of building as an increase, but to build something new, sometimes the old has to be torn away.

Palms 23 begins with a powerful promise: *"The Lord is my shepherd; I shall not want"* (NASB). This means He is our protection and provider. When life gets out of hand, when things break down, when our possessions are stripped away, when tragedy strikes all around, God is with us. He will take care of us during the crisis, and when the time is right, if we dare, He will help us build again. His desire is to write a story of victory over our lives.

No matter how many stand with us or how many flee, God remains. He is faithful. If we lack enough resources, He will step in. And as we'll see in the next chapter, when life knocks us down, He not only helps us get back up, but He gives us the strength to run toward all we were made for.

I D.A.R.E. YOU TO BUILD

Decide: Put your trust in the Lord and allow God to help you begin again, even when it means putting everything you have built at the foot of the cross.

Allow: Let God order your steps, which can feel very uncomfortable at first. But if you listen and obey His instructions, He will build your courage and strength. Through Him, you will experience ultimate victory.

Rise: Know that your victory is not found in your strength, but in your Savior. Ask Him to build your faith, knowing that faith makes way for God's favor. Plant the seeds and watch your miracle grow.

Enjoy: Bask in the knowledge that we don't have to fear, because God is our provider. He will do more with a little than we can do with much.

Chapter 14

RUN AGAIN

Carlos and I were so excited. A few years into our marriage, we had moved into the cutest house. With three lush acres and a long, winding driveway, inside and out, our cozy little place felt like home. There was just one thing missing.

We needed a new television. I wanted a small one, so it wouldn't take up most of the space in our living room. But Carlos insisted on a large screen—for his sports, of course. He loves me, but you know he won that battle.

We went to the store, and they loaded the TV into the back of our Jeep, then we headed home. But once we arrived, we discovered a problem, one the two of us couldn't handle alone. The box was extremely heavy, and more than we could carry. So Carlos said he'd ask his brother to help us.

We left the door of the Jeep open and went into the house. Neither one of us thought our four-year-old son might wander out. But you know he did.

Gabriel tried to climb inside the car door and the TV fell on top of him, pinning one of his legs. His high-pitched scream sent us racing out of the house.

We scooped him up together, and Carlos eased our son and me inside the car, before running to get behind the steering wheel.

I held Gabe on my lap, rocking and praying, while Carlos slammed the gas pedal to the floor. We arrived at the hospital in minutes.

The doctors came into the exam room and ordered X-rays. A few hours later, Gabe rode a wheelchair to our car, casted leg propped, so his crushed ankle could get adequate blood flow. We were devastated.

Gabe wore a cast for months. When they finally cut it off, life did not return to normal. Our little boy had to learn to walk again, but his issues didn't stop there.

Years later, we realized Gabe's foot and knee hadn't healed straight. As a teenager, he couldn't run without pain. Our doctor recommended a simple surgery, but I wasn't sure, nervous that something might go wrong. Unfortunately, my intuition proved right.

After the surgery, Gabe couldn't walk and lethargically laid on the sofa. These were uncommon behaviors for our previously energetic, teenaged boy. Doctors told us Gabe was suffering from septic shock—his body was fighting a severe infection that spread through his bloodstream. My son's life was in danger.

Gabe was treated with strong antibiotics and had several more surgeries. He healed slowly, but finally improved. Months and much practice later, as a new summer approached, he began to walk again.

Gabe begged me to go to the kids' church camp. Even though I knew our staff would watch over him, I felt hesitant. But he pleaded, reminding me of how long he had been cooped up, and with those beautiful brown eyes, he wore me down. I just couldn't say no—but teenager or not, he was still my baby, so I attended the camp every day except Thursday, when I drove home to check on my youngest son, Victor. I had just settled in, when the phone rang.

I could tell it was the camp counselor's voice, but I couldn't make out a word she was saying. I said, "Calm down, I can't understand you. Whatever is going on will be okay. Tell me what's going on."

I heard her inhale deeply. She hiccupped while she said, "Some of our kids were hit by a drunk driver, while sitting in the back of a car. The other car swerved and hit some of our kids."

My heart sank. I pleaded with God in my mind, *Not Gabriel. Please God, he's been through so much. Not him.*

But then the counselor confirmed my worst nightmare. "One of them was yours."

It didn't take Carlos and me long to get there.

My Gabe was lying on the ground, covered in blood on his right side. There was so much blood that initially, they couldn't tell where it was coming from. Later, we discovered he was bleeding from his elbow.

They rushed him to the hospital. We sped all the way to Charlottesville, Virginia. We actually beat the ambulance there from Richmond.

Gabe put on a brave face for the ambulance crew and hospital staff, but the minute mom walked in the room, he began to cry. Seeing him sob like he did when he was four years old, now as a six-foot-three-inch teenager, made me feel like I couldn't breathe. I couldn't believe this was happening. We were finally seeing light after a season of so much darkness. Why, now?

After many tests, the doctor came to Gabe's room to talk to us. "There's nothing we can do about this arm," he said. "Unfortunately, we have no choice but to sew him up and hope for the best. We'll send you home for now, but come back on Thursday for surgery."

I wept all the way from the hospital to our front door. This could not be happening.

That night, Gabe laid on the sofa groaning and weeping. I stayed up with him, searching the Internet for a specialist. My eyes burned and blurred from the tears that fell on my phone, but my research paid off.

Early in the morning, I called just as the doctor's office opened. He was a specialist known for repairing the mangled arms of athletes. He took my call, listened compassionately to Gabe's story, and then broke my heart. "I'm sorry, Mrs. Rivera. I can't help Gabriel, since he's a minor."

Feeling desperate, I raised my voice and begged. "He may be thirteen, but he is six-foot-three and weighs 200 pounds. He needs a man's doctor."

"I'm sorry, Mrs. Rivera." At least the doctor kindly referred me to a pediatrician before hanging up.

While I waited for the scheduled appointment with the pediatrician, I prayed for a miracle. But I confess that by the time we entered her office, utter discouragement covered me like a dark cloud. When she walked in, my first impression was not good: She seems so young. How can she possibly help my boy? My heart felt like it was falling out of my chest.

"Lay back and relax your body, Gabe," she commanded gently.

I felt like I was suffocating. "Do you need me for a minute? I have to use the restroom."

Her smile spoke softness and understanding. "We'll be fine," she patted my son's good shoulder. "It will take me a few minutes to assess Gabe anyway."

I excused myself and ran down the hall.

I saw an empty room, far enough away where my son wouldn't hear me cry. I sat on the chair and gave in to my grief. I let my tears speak the words I wasn't willing to say to God. But I didn't stay there long. Even though I didn't have any faith in her, I still wanted to hear the pediatrician's opinion of Gabe's condition.

I stopped at a bathroom and freshened my makeup. Then, with resolve, I returned Gabe's room. He was sitting upright on the exam table, looking calm.

The doctor turned toward me and said, "Rosalinda, I want you to know I will do my best for Gabriel. I follow your ministry and love what you do. My mother shops at your thrift store regularly. She says it makes her happy buying there, knowing it supports your women's home."

I felt like God was saying, "See? I'm with you. I haven't taken my eyes off of you and your family. I am in control of this. Hold onto me."

As we prepared to leave, the pediatrician scheduled a surgical procedure to work on Gabe's messed up arm. She said, "I promise, if I can't fix his arm once I'm in surgery, I will call in another doctor."

My faith in her increased. My faith in God blew up.

I called Gloria, a beautiful African-American prayer warrior from my church. I needed someone who would plug into the power of God, trusting with me that this would be Gabe's last procedure.

The day of the surgery, Gloria joined me at the hospital. After they took Gabe to the operating room, Gloria and I stayed in his hospital room, circled it, and prayed, speaking God's promises back to Him, out loud.

"Psalm 41:3: *The* LORD *nurses them when they are sick and restores them to health*" (NLT).

"Isaiah 53:5: *But he was wounded for our transgressions, he was bruised for our iniquities; the chastisement of our peace was upon him; and with his stripes we are healed*" (ASV).

"Malachi 4:2: *But for you who fear my name, the Sun of Righteousness will rise with healing in his wings. And you will go free, leaping with joy like calves let out to pasture*" (NLT).

"James 5:15: *Such a prayer offered in faith, will heal the sick, and the Lord will make you well. And if you have committed any sins, you will be forgiven*" (NLT).

"1 Peter 2:24: *He personally carried our sins in his body on the cross so that we can be dead to sin and live for what is right. By his wounds you are healed*" (NLT).

Gloria and I walked together, united in the belief that the one who created Gabe could repair him. We trusted God to have mercy on him. We committed our love and obedience to God, no matter what. And we didn't stop for hours until they brought my boy back to the room.

The pediatrician followed behind and approached me upon entering Gabe's room. "I was hoping I could take care of Gabriel myself, but as promised, I had two specialists on stand-by in case. I had to call them in."

When she told me their names, I was astounded. One of them was the sports specialist who said he couldn't work on a minor. God had given me my miracle.

I realized the pediatrician was still talking, and tuned in to hear what she had to say. "We did not have to replace his elbow with a prostheses, but he will have a metal rod and screws. It's a good outcome, but he'll only have limited use of that arm."

Hours of faith-filled prayer infused my response. I said, "No! I believe God is going to restore my son's arm." You know us mamas, when it comes to our kids, we are going to step out in faith.

The pediatrician smiled and said, "I hope you're right, Rosalinda. I hope you're right."

Gabriel worked hard during his months of therapy and recovery. As he grew stronger physically, he also bulked up spiritually. He told me more than once, "I feel closer to the Lord than ever, Mom. I realize that if the enemy was so busy trying to take me out, God must have a big plan for my life."

Gabe began to search his heart for his purpose and decided to commit his heart to God. The faith Carlos and I expressed was no longer enough. Our son realized that God was his own personal source and strength.

I never smiled wider than when Gabriel became the MVP of his high school basketball team the following season. His arm was restored, as was his leg from years before. My boy was free to shoot hoops and run again. What he did with his freedom, however, was his choice.

Thankfully, Gabe made a wise decision. He dove into his calling from God and began to lead small groups of younger teens. By age seventeen, the pastors of our church asked him to become one of the leaders of our children's church program. He was soon preaching to nearly a hundred children on a regular basis.

Gabriel's decisions make this mother's heart melt. He could have stumbled through life, allowing bitterness and unanswered questions to dominate his thoughts. But instead, he chose to believe God and overcome.

Why did Gabe endure so much at a young age? Only God knows.

After surviving sepsis that jeopardized his life, why did he have to get hit by that car? Only God knows.

WHY ARE SOME HEALED WHILE OTHERS ARE NOT? ONLY GOD KNOWS.

Why are some healed while others are not? Only God knows.

But I do believe standing on God's promises and daring to believe them make a difference. They did for my son's survival and restoration. However, while we were going through all those hard things, no one in our family reacted perfectly. No one was exercising a walk-on-water faith.

PETER UNDERSTANDS OUR NEED FOR FAITH

Peter could probably speak to some of the things we felt in our raw, human moments.

Matthew 14:22–33 tells a fascinating story. Jesus told His disciples to take a boat to the other side of the sea without Him, while He stayed behind to pray on the mountain. That night, they were still a considerable distance from shore and the sea was rough when Jesus started to walk on the water toward them. "It's a ghost!" the disciples cried.

"But Jesus immediately said to them: 'Take courage! It is I. Don't be afraid'" (Matthew 14:27).

Peter showed courage in his reply. "Lord, if it's you, tell me to come to you on the water."

Jesus's answer may have stunned Peter for a split-second. "Come," the Lord said.

The Bible tells us Peter got out of the boat, walked on the water himself, and went toward Jesus.

Picture this. The boat is being tossed by strong winds and sea waves while two men are standing on the water. Un.Be.Liev.Able!

Yet, with God, all things ARE possible. He is able!

Then, Peter realized how strong the wind was and he became afraid. Instantly, he started to sink. "Lord, save me," Peter cried out.

Jesus reached out His hand and caught Peter. "You of little faith, why did you doubt?" He asked.

> ## WHY DO WE DOUBT? IF WE'RE HONEST, IT HAPPENS TO ALL OF US SOMETIMES.

Why do we doubt? I think if we're honest, it happens to all of us sometimes, especially when something scary strikes the people we love the most.

Many of us will struggle with depression, anxiety, nightmares, discouragement, and other emotions triggered by deep fears, at least during one season of our lives. I battled those things when I feared for my Gabe. If I'm being totally transparent, there were times that Gabe's faith was stronger than mine.

But Gabe learned to keep his eyes on Jesus when the storms of life raged around him. He discovered that Christ offered him enough strength to walk on top of fluid circumstances. Gabe even dared to run again.

Today, he is studying to be a pastor at a Bible college in Alabama.

Gabe's old injuries still bring him occasional discomfort. And the eight-inch scar on his arm symbolizes life's ability to change in a moment. But every day, my son makes a choice to move forward. He walks in victory. He runs in the truth of God's promises.

> *But those who trust in the Lord will find new strength. They will soar high on wings like eagles. They will run and not grow weary. They will walk and not faint.*   (Isaiah 40:31 NLT)

What has stifled your forward motion? Make a decision in this moment to stubbornly refuse to let anything hold you back. Dare to run again. You can even fly if you choose.

What if the thing you most fear is having your heart broken again? Is it really safe to love? Let's see what God says about it in the next chapter.

I D.A.R.E. YOU TO RUN

Decide: Are you walking and running in God's favor? Or are you sinking beneath the waters of doubt, pushed by the winds of fear? Choose to believe in God's promises. Even if you don't feel faith, exercise it until your feelings begin to follow.

Allow: Our Savior will reach out and catch you, if you will only call. Cry out to Jesus, and let Him lift you above your fears.

Rise: Your scars need not define you. We all have some. Stop letting symbols of your past keep you down. Instead, use them as catapults to lift you above, to the place where all things are possible and God is able.

Enjoy: You were made to live strong. God gave you wings to soar like an eagle. He created your feet to walk. He made your legs to run. Celebrate every inch of who you are, just as God does.

Chapter 15

LOVE AGAIN

Love runs much deeper than a simple encounter. But not all love interests offer the same value.

As a young Christian, I met a wonderful young man who I thought was my prince charming. At first, he was attentive and sweet, and I felt treasured. His sensitive spirit drew me and I was captured by his affectionate ways. But little by little, a change emerged. I soon discovered that he wasn't quite who I thought he was. It took a while before I realized I'd been duped.

As we spent more time together, little by little, this boy's past hurts began to shape how he treated me. Not only was I paying for someone else's sins from a previous relationship, but I began to realize his true personality differed from what he originally displayed.

Anytime I expressed happiness, he shot it down. If I celebrated something good, he found something bad to say. If I liked a movie, he hated it. His negativity overshadowed my joy, and his dark spirit began to affect mine. Others saw the change in me before I recognized it in myself.

I waged war against what I felt. A truth tried to seep out of my soul, but I pushed back, burying it deep. After all, I convinced myself, he must be the one. I mean, he loved the Lord, his family embraced me, all seemed as it should be—or so it appeared to me.

Every once in a while, I heard a quiet voice whisper into my mind, *This is not My will. Free yourself from this relationship.*

In reality, I knew this relationship was taking me further away from my relationship with God. Several months in, I felt trapped, depressed, and anxious. I could see no way out.

But in 1 Corinthians 10:13, the Bible says God will provide a way of escape—and that He did. He opened a door I hadn't expected, but He left it up to me to walk through. If I wanted my freedom, I had to exercise my free will to get it.

I did, without hesitation. I may be slow, but I'm not dense. I jumped at the opportunity to attend college in another state.

As soon as I hit the road, my spirit lifted with an overpowering sense of lightness. It's amazing how an entrapment hides the bondage you're really in.

> IT'S AMAZING HOW AN ENTRAPMENT HIDES THE BONDAGE YOU'RE REALLY IN.

For such a long time, I had justified the relationship. I even played the savior part: If I leave him, he might do something crazy. He'll step back from going to church, or maybe even worse.

There was no denying that being with this guy had me stuck. I had stopped using my God-given gift for singing. I no longer participated in praise and worship. I wasn't doing the things God had made me to do. I allowed a toxic relationship to take me away from my purpose and God's plan. I wasn't letting God write my story.

Isn't it amazing how we can put ourselves in God's place without realizing we've done it? When I reflect back now, imagining what my life would have looked like if I'd married this guy, I know how different things would be today. And not in a good way.

It wasn't easy walking away from that situation. But it would have been much harder if I hadn't obeyed God when He told me to do it. I would have wasted years of my life, if not all of it. And I would have missed out on something much better...although in the beginning, God's plan didn't look that great to me.

I came home from college one summer and did my usual things. I hung out with my friends, spent time with my family, worked in our ministry, and participated in church activities. You know, this girl was just having a little fun.

I especially enjoyed one thing in particular. A group of us from church went to the gym in the evenings. I developed a mean racquetball game and when I was on the team, we were pretty tough to beat. But there was one opposing crew that seemed set on establishing themselves as champions. Well, I wasn't having any of that. Anyone who knows me understands I'm always up for some good competition. Bring it on—this chick's ready to take you down!

There was one guy on that team who rubbed me like sandpaper going against the grain on wood. He'd gotten saved at our church, and honestly, I didn't care for him that much. After all, saved people are still people. And some personalities clash. I thought he was hot-headed, stuck on himself, and apparently believed he was God's gift to women.

The more he mouthed off, the more determined I was to put him in his place. And the racquetball court was perfect for that. I decided beating him would shut him up.

Actually, I'd known him for years. Our families were friends, but he had always teased me and given me a hard time. However, I wasn't a kid anymore, and I'd had enough.

Many nights that summer, Carlos and I played racquetball within our church group. Over sweaty battles and blistering taunts, we spent more and more time together. We also helped behind the scenes at a local revival, where my dad was the guest speaker.

On and off the court, Carlos pushed my buttons, and the more he did it, the more I disliked him. But I guess God sees things in people that we often don't. So do dads.

One evening, on our way to a restaurant after church, my father said, "Rosalinda, why don't you let Carlos come with us?"

I thought, *Dad, you've got to be out of your mind.* But I didn't want to make waves. So Carlos joined us and I tried not to sulk.

But as we sat there with my entire family, the jokes started flowing. I don't know when I stopped pouting and starting having fun, but before I knew it, I was laughing so much my stomach hurt. We stayed in the restaurant so long, it was after 1:00 a.m. before we all got home.

The next day, Carlos showed up and asked me if I'd like to hang out. I must admit, this time I didn't feel quite as repulsed as I did before. And when his arm or leg accidentally brushed mine, I felt sparks. What was going on?

After that, Carlos began showing up "just to hang out" again and again. I started looking forward to his arrival and even spent some extra time sprucing myself up in the mornings.

Somehow, as the weeks progressed, Carlos's taunting didn't bother me like it used to, and I rather enjoyed dishing it right back. I realized he had become much more than my racquetball opponent; we now competed over who could "one up" the other. Only now, it felt less frustrating and more like flirting.

Carlos Rivera had captured my heart. But our blossoming love had some challenges. I imagined people in our church and community would say, "They're crazy to think it will work." But I was crazy in love.

On our first formal date, Carlos asked me to go with him to a Fourth of July celebration. We weren't telling anyone about us yet, not even our church family. So we decided to go to an event we thought they weren't attending. I told Carlos, "I still don't think they're ready for us."

As dusk fell and the fireworks were getting ready to begin, Carlos fanned a soft blanket on the ground for us to share. We nestled in close, though not too intimately, and opened the picnic basket we'd brought. I was enjoying his presence and anticipating the fireworks, when he leaned near my ear. I shivered in a good way.

"Don't look now, but I think the entire church is sitting behind us."

I tried to look without looking like I was looking, but it was pointless. I had to twist my neck and turn my head. At the gotcha grins from the small group behind us, there was no denying we were busted. So we laughed in good humor and got back to our special celebration.

When Carlos suggested salsa dancing for our second date, I was not down for that. All I could think about was the scandal if someone saw us. Getting busted having a picnic at a fireworks display was one thing, but getting caught doing the cha cha or merengue was a different deal.

I imagined the whispers if we were spotted by someone from our church: Look, it's our worship leader and the pastor's kid doing salsa!

But Carlos was convincing. "Come on, Rosalinda, no one from church will be there. They're not going to be out doing salsa. You're young—let go and live while you can."

I finally caved and we went. Our second date took place on a Friday night.

On Sunday morning, Carlos and I made sure we kept our distance from each other and tried to avoid eye contact. We wanted our relationship to stay low-key. At least for now. But I must admit, after doing salsa with him, it was super hard not to look his way.

Almost twenty-five years later, I can tell you, he's still got moves.

On that Sunday, we both walked into church like nothing was up, but the looks we were getting said something was sideways.

I tried to reassure myself. It's just in your head. Your guilt is getting the best of you. No one from the church was there, you watched to make sure. But my paranoia wasn't helped by the nudges and whispers every time someone looked at one of us. We soon found out what was really going on.

The Sunday morning paper ran a front page story about the salsa event. And guess whose picture was dead center below the byline? Me and my not-so-secret man, heads thrown back in laughter, moving to the beat.

Even after the paper outed us, Carlos and I both felt protective and respectful of our church family. We wanted to ease into things before we made any public announcements or stepped out too much as a couple, so we took our time.

As our relationship deepened, I reflected. When I'd struggled with letting go of my former relationship, I had no idea God would put someone in my life who I could love so much. I didn't know when I was in the middle of that pain that I would laugh again—and actually laugh much more than I had before. I almost missed God's best by thinking I knew what it was without consulting Him.

I ALMOST MISSED GOD'S BEST BY THINKING I KNEW WHAT IT WAS WITHOUT CONSULTING HIM.

Sometimes, we assume something is from God, when it has nothing to do with His plan at all. Then our hearts are crushed by the hurt we've brought on ourselves. By then, we often feel stuck or worse. One bad relationship is all it takes to make us swear off love forever.

But you may be reading this and thinking, *Your story's sweet and all, but you have no idea what I've walked through. You don't know the betrayal I've felt. You don't know the wounds inflicted on me. You have no idea what real loss feels like.*

If any of this rings true for you, please understand that although I may not know exactly how you feel, if we share long enough, most of us will discover an emotional connection due to some similarity in circumstances. We all have stories.

For instance, I have no idea exactly how Mary, the mother of Jesus, felt when she was forced to watch her son die on the cross for us. And He did so in an excruciating way. Let's see if we can put ourselves in Mary's shoes.

MARY WATCHED HELPLESSLY AS JESUS WAS CRUCIFIED

In a minute part of Scripture, John 19:25–27, we see the most exquisite picture of love ever painted. Jesus has chosen not to fight His crucifixion. He is going to die for our sins. His mother stood by helplessly as His blood dripped off the wood, spilling onto the ground.

The Bible doesn't tell us much about her emotional state, but I think it's safe to guess. Mary had changed Jesus's swaddling clothes, prepared His food, kissed His skinned knees, and held Him for hugs. But as He hung nearly naked, hungry, beaten, and bloodied, she could not comfort her wounded child. Oh, how her soul must have ached, knowing He would soon draw His final breath—and she could not trade places with Him, nor could she stop it.

But Jesus looked down and saw her pain. When He did, Mary wasn't entirely alone, though she must have felt that way.

Christ looked at her, and also at the disciple He loved standing next to her. Jesus said to Mary, "Dear woman, here is your son." And to the disciple, he said, "Here is your mother."

After this exchange, the disciple took Mary into his home. In essence, Jesus obtained a new son for Mary. But can you replace the greatest love of your life? I can think of only one way—by allowing God to write the rest of your story.

Heaven is a real place. And when I consider what Mary faced as her Son hung from a rough-hewn tree, she too must have believed in heaven. Of all the human beings who ever lived, Mary most of all would have accepted Jesus Christ as her personal savior. For her, it was extremely personal. This gave her the hope and assurance of a heavenly reunion with her son. Until they were reunited, she would have to give herself permission to love again.

> IF WE DARE TO LOVE JESUS, WE CAN HAVE THE SAME HOPE AND ASSURANCE AS MARY.

If we dare to love Jesus, we can have the same hope and assurance as Mary. And regardless of what we've lost here on earth, we can experience love again, if we are willing to accept it.

Jesus showed us what real, absolute, unconditional, no-matter-what love looks like. But He is also the Way, the Truth, and the Life, offering us access to heaven. No matter what we lose on earth, we have an opportunity to regain it and then some, in eternity, when God writes our entire story.

So many people put up emotional walls, meant to keep other people out.

+ We assume things about people, like I did with Carlos at first, without giving them a chance to show us who they really are.

- We blame people for situations, without listening to what they have to say.

- We project behaviors from past betrayals onto our current loves, without seeing if our actions are appropriate.

- We blame God when someone is taken away, pushing away the pen of His promise in our anger and pain.

Shutting our hearts down and refusing to love again is a tragedy we can avoid. God desires our restoration and He will write it into our story, if we let Him turn the page. When we dare to love again, we learn to live again, so we can begin again.

Throughout this book, I have challenged you in many areas. God is definitely continuing to write your story. Be courageous and allow Him to pen His promises on your life.

We have one final topic to cover. I believe it is the most powerful piece necessary for truly beginning again. Join me, as we express our gratitude and turn the final pages toward complete healing. It IS possible to begin again. Your next chapter awaits.

I D.A.R.E. YOU TO LOVE

Decide: Love is not a fuzzy thing that merely happens to you. It comes when you choose to look for and see the best in someone else. If you focus only on a feeling, you can miss out on some of the greatest love moments of your life.

Allow: God will clarify any confusing questions you may have about love. But you must have an attentive heart, listening ear, patient spirit, and open eyes to see His answers. Unlocking your mind is the only way to see His truth.

Rise: Betrayal, hurt, and loss are part of the package when you seek love in the wrong places. Rise beyond your desire for immediate gratification. Allow God's best to take you higher than you've ever been before.

Enjoy: Too often, love is all around us, but we take our loved ones for granted. We focus on their flaws instead of their fabulous traits. We put them down instead of building them up. We forget why we loved them in the first place as we nag them for a perceived current failure. Every day of your life, decide to delight in those you love. It's the gift you give away that will cause your own cup to overflow.

Chapter 16

THANK AGAIN

Odds are, you have experienced one or more of the following:

+ Life has blindsided you, knocking you off course. You weren't asked permission for circumstances to kick you in the gut.

+ You've taken a wrong turn and made a decision you wish you could take back.

+ On the heels of one of the above, you feel stuck. It seems as if you've run out of gas and no matter what you do, you can't find the fuel to move beyond stumbling through your days in survival mode.

Now that you've gotten to know me better, you understand how I can relate to the first two. Recently, however, I went through something that could be described as either sad or funny, depending on how you look at it. But it also draws a picture of what can happen to us when we feel stuck.

The honking began immediately, and the cursing soon followed. My car would not budge. No matter how many times I turned the key or hit the gas pedal, it refused to move. The worst part was my location. I was out of gas in the middle of a major intersection on Midlothian Turnpike, a busy thoroughfare in Virginia.

Heat rose from my neck and flushed across my cheeks as enraged drivers shouted.

"Get out of the way."

"Move that piece of junk."

"Come on, you stupid witch."

I've cleaned up their language to give you the pretty version, but you get my point. I was stuck. And even though I wanted nothing more than to move on and forget the situation ever happened, I was helpless to change anything on my own.

This had never happened to me before, although it easily could have. In my car, even though the gas gauge shows empty, I know there is really fuel left in the tank. On other occasions, I've pushed my car past its normal limits and driven for a whole extra day. I don't recommend it, but from experience, I can tell you it's possible. And now that I write this, I realize that my daredevil driving ways likely landed me in a stuck place.

I have this habit that's a little embarrassing to admit, in light of the situation I just described. But we're friends here, right? I know my vehicle so well that I can look at my gas gauge and tell when my car's about to die, allowing me to maneuver myself to the nearest pump. Just in time.

Many times, I've taken pride in my ability to score gas right at the final second. Obviously, I played the game a little too tight this time. Intersection 1; Rosalinda 0.

When this happened, I saw no signs, nor did I receive any advance warnings that I recognized. I was caught by surprise. My Chevy had had enough. At 5:00 p.m. rush hour. On a Monday. In intense summer heat. It died.

I called AAA and they gave me their ETA. I was going to endure a lot more road rage before my situation improved. I was stuck.

But then, I looked in my rearview mirror and caught a glimpse of something I didn't expect. Someone I knew had pulled up behind me.

My friend and New Life For Youth co-worker, Victoria, happened to be driving in the area. She recognized my car and immediately got out to assist. She suggested we call our ministry car shop for help. Now why didn't I think of that?

Within minutes, a couple of our guys showed up with a full gas can. They poured the fuel into my Chevy, then turned the key. But still no go.

One of the guys popped the hood, allowing the other to duck underneath it. Then they put their heads together, conferring over my stubborn and rebellious car. I stood helplessly to the side. I shuffled my feet, while I tried not to make eye contact with the frustrated drivers who continued to yell and offer hand gestures as they routed around us.

Finally, the guys figured out that by letting my car run completely out of gas, I had ruined the fuel filter. They ran down the street, bought one, installed it, put some more gas in my car, and tried the key once more. Sweet relief flooded my veins when the engine turned over and began to purr. Because they helped me get unstuck, I could begin driving again.

> I PUSHED MYSELF TO THE LIMIT AND LOST CONTROL.

I learned a priceless lesson at a high cost that day. I discovered the foolishness of waiting to fill my car because of an arrogant game I played with myself. I pushed myself to the limit and lost control. I experienced the humiliation of costing others unnecessary interruptions in their day— other drivers, my friends, and co-workers—not to mention the people whose schedules were delayed because of me. I set myself up for the painful moment of standing in that busy intersection. The insults people hurled at me came because I made a stubborn and rebellious decision earlier. I paid the price of pointless expenses by not taking care of things when I should have.

I had to buy a new fuel filter because I dragged my feet and did not get gas when I should have. Once I got myself stuck, I couldn't get myself out on my own. I needed a rescue from someone who knew what it would take to save me.

Before it was possible to move beyond the situation, someone had to identify and correct the true source of my issue. If I couldn't do it by myself, I had to be smart enough to recognize it and wise enough to accept the help I needed. Then I needed to refuel as a means for driving. I need a catalyst to help me move past the pain.

Throughout this book, we've seen how prone we all are to making decisions that get us stuck. We can become immobilized when life hits us in the gut. Sometimes, the two are connected.

But whether we've done something stubborn and rebellious, acted arrogantly, and played dangerous games, or were innocently slammed by something unforeseen, God sees what we're going through. If we take a wrong turn, God is there. If we pass the gas station, thinking we'll refuel later, God is there. If we are stranded in the middle of an intersection, God is there. If we need a rescuer, God is there.

> IF WE ARE STRANDED IN THE MIDDLE OF AN INTERSECTION, GOD IS THERE. IF WE NEED A RESCUER, GOD IS THERE.

Your story doesn't have to end where you were in the past or where you are now. God will add new chapters to your life, filled with fresh hope, renewed encouragement, and new motivation. If you look up, you might even find He is writing a friend into the scene. But for every clean slate, for us to begin again, I believe we need something specific to fuel us forward. If you want to move out of your rut and get unstuck, it's essential.

When I've felt hurt or discouraged, I've been inspired by reading what others have said about gratitude.

"The more you express gratitude for what you have, the more things you'll have to express gratitude for."
—Zig Ziglar

"Gratitude turns what you have into enough."
—Melody Beattie

"Let gratitude be the pillow upon which you kneel to say your nightly prayer." —Dr. Maya Angelou

"Gratitude is the fairest blossom which springs from the soul." —Henry Ward Beecher

"The grateful person knows that God is good, not by hearsay but by experience." —Thomas Merton

Intentional gratitude, daring to be thankful, is the best strategy for giving yourself the drive so you can dare to begin again. And one more quote speaks to the importance of being intentional in order to be successfully grateful.

Andy Stanley says, "None of us plan—or intend—to get into trouble. The problem is, we don't plan not to."

THANKFULNESS IS THE FUEL THAT FEEDS OUR MINDS, BODIES, AND SPIRITS WITH RENEWED GET UP AND GO.

I believe practicing intentional gratitude means planning for it daily so you will act on it daily. When we are running on empty, feeling frustrated, overwhelmed, and tired, thankfulness is the fuel that feeds our minds, bodies, and spirits with renewed get up and go. It's the high octane energy available to us every day. But we have to ensure we don't get so busy or arrogant that we drive right by it.

There's another crucial reason we should exercise intentional gratitude. When we express thanksgiving for the small gifts in our here and now, it impacts our trustworthiness. God can write more of our story.

How do I make that connection? Because people take care of what they are grateful for. And God speaks to this in the Bible. Jesus told His disciples:

> *One who is faithful in a very little is also faithful in much, and one who is dishonest in a very little is also dishonest in much. If then you have not been faithful in the unrighteous wealth, who will entrust to you the true riches? And if you have not been faithful in that which is another's, who will give you that which is your own?*   (Luke 16:10–12 ESV)

In other words, if you can be trusted with a little, you can be trusted with a lot. And if you are grateful for a little, God will give you more.

Gratitude moves us beyond our past or present situations into something better.

Thanksgiving is the foundation from which God writes the best parts of our stories. And He did that with Paul.

THROWN INTO PRISON, PAUL PRAISED GOD

Paul's story in Acts 16:16 starts innocently enough. He and Silas are going to a place of prayer, minding their own business, when a young, possessed fortune-teller starts following them and shouting, *"These men are servants of the Most High God, who proclaim to you the way of salvation"* (Acts 16:17 ESV).

Now, that might not have bothered Paul and Silas so much, except she didn't do this just once. This girl followed them around for many days, crying out the same thing over and over. Think about a time when someone kept telling you the same thing repeatedly. It gets on your nerves, right?

Apparently, Paul had enough. He finally turned to her and said to the spirit, "'*I command you in the name of Jesus Christ to come out of her.' And it came out that very hour*" (Acts 16:18 ESV). But that's when Paul's real trouble started.

This girl was a slave and her owners weren't happy that her fortune-telling powers left with the spirit that possessed her. So they had Paul and Silas arrested on trumped up charges. The two disciples were beaten and thrown into prison, with their feet shackled.

How would you have felt if you were Paul? Have you ever been stalked or harassed by someone? Has someone lied, exaggerated, dramatized, or accused you unfairly? Have people ever ganged up on you? Have you felt stuck?

Do any of these descriptions fit your life now?

If so, then Paul is a good example of someone who really gets you. It's a real challenge to follow his example in this situation. Instead of complaining about being in that dark, dirty prison, he and Silas prayed and sang praises to God.

Then something incredible happened. There was a great earthquake, shaking the prison foundations. Immediately, all the doors were opened and all the prisoners were free.

By expressing gratitude when all appeared hopeless, when being thankful looked a little bit crazy, Paul connected to the power of God's Spirit. That's when relief came. Whew! See, God doesn't promise to make sense to us. He promises that if we dare to believe Him, He will set us free.

PRAISE IS GRATITUDE IN ACTION

My dear friend, God wants to remove the shackles off your life. The reason and the story behind your emotional imprisonment may not be fair. But through the ultimate sacrifice of God's Son, Jesus, you can be made whole.

All the injustices, everything bad that ever happened to you, all the mistakes you've made, every unfair and deep wound that has shaped you into the person you are, and every broken piece of your life can be redeemed. The price has been paid by Jesus. He loves you so much that He gave up His life and said, "Forgive them."

Though He knew no sin, He was beaten and bruised for you. He wore a crown of thorns upon His head, so that you would not have to bear the crown of hurt, anxiety, and brokenness.

All things are possible for you—if you will dare to begin again.

Walk in the freedom set before you. You are no longer a slave to sin, your past, your hurts, or your emotions. They need not control you. You are a child of God, redeemed and loved. Refuse to let your circumstances distance you from God's presence. Dare to thank Him again.

> YOU ARE A CHILD OF GOD, REDEEMED AND LOVED.

Psalm 100 reminds us to enter into God's presence with thanksgiving. If you begin to thank Him for waking you up each day, for giving you life, for giving you hope, your life will begin to change. Gratitude gives us endurance. A grateful person is a happy person. Ask the Lord to help you become grateful.

In the Bible, there are many examples of people who had to start again. But their fresh slate began with a decision. We've reviewed them throughout our time together.

+ The man at the Pool of Bethesda dared to begin again.

+ Naomi dared to dream again.

+ The man in the graveyard dared to release again.

+ Daniel dared to hope again.

+ Joseph dared to forgive again.

+ Jonah dared to listen again.

+ Jochebed dared to sacrifice again.

+ Jacob dared to risk again.

+ Hannah dared to believe again.

+ David dared to trust again.

+ The Samaritan woman dared to connect again.

+ Lazarus dared to heal again.

+ Gideon dared to build again.

+ Peter dared to run again.

+ Mary, the mother of Jesus, dared to love again.

+ And Paul dared to thank again.

So I ask you, what will it take for you to dare? Remember, God is still writing your story. He desires nothing more than to bring it to a satisfying conclusion. You see, when He pens "The End" on your final earthly chapter, He wants to start your never-ending story in eternity. Allow Jesus to pen His promise over your life. Let Him restore you. Dare to thank Him, as you take that first step and dare to begin again.

I D.A.R.E. YOU TO THANK

Decide: Intentional gratitude will change your life. Choose to look for things you can feel thankful for. Praise God for your favorite flavor of ice cream, the clean air you breathe, or the special smile you just received.

Allow: Put three thankful things down on paper every day. Let gratitude seep into and soak through the very fiber of who you are. Do not put a wall around your grateful heart. Instead, tear down walls and allow gratefulness to infuse every cell of your being.

Rise: Everything that you have ever experienced has happened to at least one other person. Don't feel sorry for yourself; refuse to justify. Instead rise beyond circumstance or situation. Pray and praise where you are. And thank God before it makes sense to do so. When you choose gratitude, He will shake things up, break those chains around your ankles, and throw the prison doors wide open. He will set you free to fly.

Enjoy: Gratitude is your most important attitude. Feel thankful for everything that shaped your character and taught you lessons. Wake up every day telling God how grateful you are. With each new morning, He waits to whisper in your ear, "I'm still writing your story. This is your chance. Begin again." Dare to enjoy your time listening to Him.

ABOUT THE AUTHOR

Rosalinda Rivera is the executive director of New Life For Youth, one of Virginia's largest residential facilities helping to rehabilitate people from a life of addiction. She has been reaching out to families in crisis, poverty, and hopelessness for over twenty-five years.

Using her business skills, Rosalinda developed a model of social enterprise to sustain the non-profit New Life For Youth by creating businesses that train thousands of young people in job skills and leadership.

She is also the president of New Life Enterprises, the founder of Mercy Moms Home, a place for single mothers to find hope and healing, and the founder of Bella Women's Ministry in Richmond, Virginia, which hosts annual conferences for over five hundred women.

Each year, Rosalinda is a featured presenter at various events nationwide. She has ministered throughout the world and has traveled to over twenty-two countries. From the White House to the local community, she has been nationally recognized for her impact in bringing hope to the hopeless.

Rosalinda was appointed to the Board of Governors of the National Association of Nonprofit Organizations & Executives, headquartered in Washington, DC. *Style Magazine* selected her as a "Top 40 under 40" leader for her impact in Richmond, Virginia.

In 2018, the Valentine Museum in Richmond will feature the work of her family as one of the city's first Hispanic families to impact Richmond in the non-profit sector.

Rosalinda is the daughter of Victor Torres, an ex-gang member from the streets of New York, and his wife, Carmen, the founders of New Life For Youth and pastors of New Life Outreach International Church. She served as an associate producer on *Victor*, a movie about her father's journey from drugs and gangs to Jesus and redemption.

Rosalinda and her husband, Carlos, have three children: Alana, Gabriel, and Victor.

Welcome to Our House!

We Have a Special Gift for You

It is our privilege and pleasure to share in your love of Christian books. We are committed to bringing you authors and books that feed, challenge, and enrich your faith.

To show our appreciation, we invite you to sign up to receive a specially selected **Reader Appreciation Gift**, with our compliments. Just go to the Web address at the bottom of this page.

God bless you as you seek a deeper walk with Him!

WE HAVE A GIFT FOR YOU. VISIT:

whpub.me/nonfictionthx

WHITAKER
HOUSE